Along The Thomasine Path

Along The Thomasine Path

❖

Rituals, Readings, and Resources for the Post-Christian, Post-Denominational Follower of Jesus.

Donald Bruce Stouder

iUniverse, Inc.
New York Lincoln Shanghai

Along The Thomasine Path
Rituals, Readings, and Resources for the Post-Christian, Post-Denominational Follower of Jesus.

iUniverse, Inc.

For information address:
iUniverse, Inc.
2021 Pine Lake Road, Suite 100
Lincoln, NE 68512
www.iuniverse.com

ISBN: 0-595-31862-2

Printed in the United States of America

For my bishop, my mentor, and my friend, the late Marcia Herndon, Ph.D.

And for Michael, a new love who has brought me new life.

Contents

Acknowledgments

I am first indebted to my fellow Thomas Christians, whose passion and strength have often provided me with inspiration. They include Rick Stanuikynas, Margaret Denvil, Billye Talmadge, Bill Fite, Phil Deming, Gerry O'Sullivan, Scott West, Anne Stewart, and Ellie Atwood-Tarbell. While I am no longer formerly connected to their community, I feel connected in Spirit. Thanks also to Gerry O'Sullivan and James Ishmael Ford for providing much of the material in the Herford and Itkin biographies. As in my last book, many of the essays that appear here where originally delivered as sermons to the nice people of Summit Unitarian Universalist Fellowship in San Diego, California. I appreciate their patience and feedback.

Liturgy and ritual are truly art forms, and I have borrowed from others to adapt the material in this work. Those sources include A New Zealand Prayer Book, The Church of the Province of New Zealand, 1989, Collins London; Handbook of Religious Services, Church of the Larger Fellowship Unitarian Universalist, 1990, Boston; Book of Worship, United Church of Christ, 1986, New York. For help in constructing the calendar of observances, I thank A Liberation Prayer Book, John Brown and Richard York, 1971, Morehouse-Barlow, New York; The Book of Common Prayer of the Syro-Chaldean Christian Community, Mikhail Itkin, 1978, San Francisco; Earth Prayers, Elizabeth Roberts and Elias Amidon, 1991, HarperSanFrancisco; and A Pilgrim's Almanac, Edward Hays, 1989, Forest of Peace Books, Topeka.

Preface

This work is a meditation, worship and reference tool for those members of the Church who call ourselves Thomas Christians. It may be used individually or in group ritual, and is meant to be a living document, that is, able to change and grow as needs or the creativity of others is expressed.

Still others may come upon this collection and find that it speaks to their own need or evolving spirituality. Such persons may rightly ask themselves, "just who are these Thomas Christians, and where did they come from?" I thought a brief statement about who we are might be helpful.

Twenty first century Thomas Christians, like their first or second century ancestors before them, are a diverse group of "itinerant radicals" who claim an ancestry that goes back to the authors of the Gospel of Thomas, and the community that existed around that gospel. In our modern incarnation, we were founded in 1901 by an English Unitarian named Vernon Herford, who sought to found an ecumenical Christian community and did so by seeking consecration as a bishop from St. Thomas Christians in India. It was another bishop, Mikhail Itkin, many decades later, who would take Herford's tradition and craft it into a social justice movement in San Francisco during the turbulent 60's and 70's. We owe virtually everything we are and stand for today to these two visionaries.

But it is individual Thomasines today that have done the most to define our mission and ministry, and to place it squarely within the most recent scholarship of the Gospel of Thomas and early Christian community. We are a group that eschews institutional religion in favor of itinerant ministries. We are not church-builders, and have no congregations save small base communities for worship and study. No Thomas Christian is supported in his or her ministry by a collection plate. Rather, we move among the world in our called ministries of service. We are hospital chaplains and counselors, nurses and educators, health care workers and justice activists. Scattered throughout the United States, it is the modern conveniences of telephone and e-mail that bind us together in community.

Although a part of the independent catholic movement in the mythical "apostolic succession", we are a community with a very loose hierarchy. When I served as convening bishop, I held an office that any member of the fellowship, including a layperson, may be elected to. I was simply a facilitator, mentor and teacher, the main function of a bishop in our fellowship, and I had no more authority than the newest seeker. Following the earliest Thomas Christians, women are included fully in every aspect of our community. And following the lead of Bishop Mikhail Itkin, who was one of the first religious leaders in the United States, and perhaps the world, to openly ordain gay and lesbian persons to the ministry, we are a community that is radically inclusive and proud of our welcoming heritage.

Theologically, we are best described as diverse. Most of our members are the products of other denominations, and so bring a wide variety of opinion, belief, and training. We welcome this intellectual and spiritual pluralism. We tend toward the liberal side of the theological spectrum, and espouse no creed or doctrine. Having said that, there are some things we can agree on, such as the creational nature of our rituals, which speak to our vision of God as being within and among all of creation and throughout the Universe, not separate-from but fully part of everything in existence. Logion 77 in the Gospel of Thomas teaches Jesus' creational theology: "I am the light that is over all things. I am all: from me all came forth, and to me all attained. Split a piece of wood; I am there. Lift up the stone, and you will find me there." Contemporary theologians who embrace creation spirituality, such as Matthew Fox, are also accurately explaining many creational views with which we would agree. In matters such as the difference between Unitarian and Trinitarian doctrine, we make no judgment and hold no opinion other than as individuals. Doctrinal distinctions such as these are ignored within the text of the Gospel of Thomas, and there is no evidence that they were of any concern to early Christian and Thomasine communities. Some of us even hold dual affiliations; like my brother bishop Vernon Herford before me, I am a Unitarian minister.

For us, the authentic teachings of the historical Jesus of Nazareth are where the rubber meets the road. It is here that Thomasine praxis becomes post-denominational and post-Christian, as the title of this work specifies. We find that the most important expression of Jesus' teachings is when we are ministering to others in pastoral roles, not in the building of institutions and in the accumulation of power. All of the rituals in this book were designed with this in mind. They help to mark the passages we all endure, the joyful and the tragic. They help to mark the circle of life. My highest wish is that you will find in them the words and poetry to help you express your deepest feelings and love for Divinity, as you experience the cycles of your own life.

San Diego, California
Summer Solstice, 2004

1

What Americans Are Thinking

We have become a country governed, controlled, and driven by public opinion polls. Courage and leadership are commodities long since evicted from our political landscape, replaced by the fickle American preoccupation with the latest survey on this issue or that issue. So I was understandably suspicious when I happened to the surfing the New York Times Magazine's web page a month or two ago and discovered an article called "With or Without a Prayer", written by Elmore Leonard. The article was one of a series analyzing a very large and well done public opinion poll called "The Way We Live Now Poll: The Inner Life of Americans Views on Spirituality, Identity, Sexuality, Anxiety, and More".

For those of you who care about such things, this was a telephone poll of a random sample of 1003 adults in all 50 states, conducted for the New York Times Magazine by Blum and Weprin Associates. The sample was based on a design which draws numbers from all existing telephone exchanges in all 50 states, giving all phone numbers, listed and unlisted, a proportionate chance of being included. Respondents were selected randomly within the household, and the results were weighted to reflect the correct demographics of the U.S. population. Error calculations demonstrated that the chances are about 19 out of 20 that if every household in America were surveyed with the same questionnaire, the complete census would not be found to deviate from the poll findings by more than 3 points. Error in subgroups might be higher, and other sources of error that can't be accounted for include question wording, question order, and interviewer effects.

So now that I have read you the fine print, what did the poll show, and why should we care? Well, I cared because it softened my heart a bit to an American population that I often find myself alienated from. It gave me hope, and demonstrated to me that, just maybe, some of the hard work of justice and compassion and nonviolence and peacemaking that we liberal churches engage in might just be paying off.

First, say the American people, no strong God, no strong rules, no strong superiors, moral or otherwise. This poll finds that most Americans want to decide for themselves what is right, good, and meaningful. I rejoice in his conclusion. Our mythical American history would have us believe that we have always admired the individualist willing to leave society behind to discover his or her true self, but for most of this century, and especially in the 1950's, Americans were only too happy to find in faith, family, or subdivision the security they needed to get through the insecurities of life.

Naturally the results, which interested me the most, were the questions about religious belief. Despite a widely perceived trend toward secularization, which church attendance seems to bear out, 49% of the respondents said they were about as religious as their parents, and 21% said they were more religious. While they may be religious, they are not theological. My own experience at virtually every social function I have ever attended, weather or not others know I am a Minister, is that doctrinal disputes leave most people bored and snoring. Americans want a loving God who smiles on everyone, not a jealous God protective of one particular franchise on Her teachings. 75% of the respondents believe in the intrinsic goodness of people, which would seem to indicate, whether they realize it or not, that they no longer subscribe to the Puritanism that has informed our national morality from the beginning, and the original sin that goes along with it. Of course, you would be hard pressed to believe this if your only source of information was our political arena or our press. But I suspect that most Americans are just as sick of that sideshow as I am, and sooner or later the media will catch on and find something else to feed us. After all, the poll seems to show that Americans tend to be cynical about politicians, distrustful of institutions, and if voting data is to be believed, very civically disengaged. Yet they feel good about themselves and their loved ones, though another source of data, the total number of drugs dispensed for anxiety, depression, or insomnia might dispute this. Still, the public and private seem to constitute two entirely different realms of life, one driven by suspicion, and the other driven by compassion. The same Americans who give to charity are more likely to support welfare reform. Many Americans who disapprove of Gays and Lesbians will respond with compassion when someone they know becomes HIV-positive. As Alan Wolfe says, "let an issue be defined as a cause, and Americans, wary of the impersonal and abstract, will turn their backs. Let it be defined as a matter of friendship, family, or faith, and they will act generously". In America, it is not the issue that matters. It is whether the issue is viewed as public or private. The public is what you have to do; the private is what you want to do. This last bit of analysis may be the most valuable insight

I took from this study. There seems to be a moral majority in America, but it just happens to be unwilling to follow anyone's party line about what morality ought to be.

If we have truly entered the age of autonomy in America, then Americans are increasingly on their own when it comes to finding the right way to live, because autonomy means different things to different people. Black Americans show less confidence that they can be anything they want to be, and are more likely than whites to conclude that those who get to the top of American society are less moral. They are also more inclined than whites to believe that race played a big role in making them who they are. As with race, so with class. The wealthiest and most educated of the respondents find fewer faults with unequal income distribution than the poorer and less educated. It helps to feel good about the world when the world has been good to you.

Certainly. America is a harder country to govern in an age of autonomy. We Americans are increasingly unwilling to do things just because someone in authority tells us we should. Everyone seems to have an opinion on truths that were once considered self-evident. But I think there are clear reasons why society is better off when people value inner autonomy. Remember I said that 90% of those surveyed said that being an American is a big part of who they are. I would like to think that this is because being an American enables us to discover who we are. Our ancestors in Puritan America, especially women and minorities, were instructed in the proper way to live, often by white men who could not live by the rules they designed for others. Compared with those eras, the age of autonomy is worth celebrating for the sense of freedom it offers. Perhaps the age of autonomy should be embraced for another reason: to me, it is an optimistic theory of human nature that makes more sense than the one it replaces. Earlier worldviews taught that a strong God, like a strong state, was needed to keep weak people in line. But Americans seem to see themselves as capable of making their way in the world without firm guidance from their moral superiors. Assuming that human beings are inherently weak or depraved does not improve our spiritual or public lives.

On the other hand, living in an age of autonomy is bound to cause frustration, because the things that matter most should matter to us all. Some Americans seem to get this; 61% think that America was a better place when people had stronger attachments and did not move around so much. This age of autonomy is bound to have its critics, and autonomy does raise the prospect of a whole nation full of people so preoccupied with their private selves to care much about the common good. But it also challenges those who emphasize the importance of the common good to listen carefully to what Americans find valuable about their way of life. As Alan Wolfe says, "the question is whether Americans can learn to use the autonomy they have gained to strengthen the institutions that make civil society possible. If they do not, this new age promises to be unstable. But if they do, it will produce institutions from which people will feel less need to escape, in large measure because institutions will not escape from them".

A significant part of what I do as a hospital chaplain is help autonomous people make important decisions about their health care, decisions that include when to allow death to be the welcome outcome. I want an age of autonomy as these decisions are made, instead of the previous age of medical professionals using their power and influence to make these decisions. And I welcome the new spiritual autonomy, which has allowed Americans to explore their inner selves as never before, and choose what they want to believe and what they want to reject. But we must always remember that there is a dark side to this age of autonomy, such as those in political or religious or even marketing circles that want control over Americans for their own ends. Autonomy requires a much higher level of vigilance than freedom ever did before. But the rewards of this new age of autonomy could be the realization of a new level of freedom for all our citizens that people like Martin Luther King Jr., describing the promised land, could only dream of.

2

Morning and Evening Meditation

A Bell may be rung.

Invocation

> My sisters and brothers, our help
> is in the name of the eternal God,

> **who co-creates with us, who is
> making the heavens and the earth.**

Silence

> Let us worship the God of love.

> **Alleluia. Alleluia.**

Psalm

*A psalm from the lectionary or another of the
leader's choosing may be said or sung here.*

Reading

*A passage of scripture or other literature is read,
followed by meditative silence.
A brief homily may be given if desired.*

Canticle

Ground Me In Your Grace, by Ted Loder

> Eternal One, Silence from whom my words come,
> Questioner from whom my questions arise,
> Lover of whom all my loves are hints,
> Disturber in whom alone I find my rest,
> Mystery in whose depths I find healing and myself;
> enfold me now in your presence,
> restore me to your peace,
> renew me through your power,
> and ground me in your grace.

The Prayers

> O God of many names, lover of all peoples;
> we pray for peace in our hearts and homes,
> in our nations and our world; the peace of
> your will, the peace of our need.

> **Dear Jesus, our friend and our**
> **guide, compassionate healer, trusted**
> **brother, passing through darkness**
> **to make it light, walk with us that**
> **we may feel your touch, and bring**
> **us to life and to community.**

Individual and corporate prayers may be offered here,
silently or aloud. Silence is kept between prayers.

> O God of peace and justice, of holiness and
> love, knit us together in mind and flesh, in
> feeling and in spirit, and make us one,
> ready for your world of love, the
> fulfillment of all our hopes, In the glory of
> our friend Jesus.

> **Keep us in the spirit of joy and**
> **simplicity and mercy. Bless us and**
> **those you have entrusted to us, in**
> **and through your many Holy Names. Amen.**

In faith and hope, we pray together....

Eternal Spirit,
Earth-maker, Pain-bearer, Life-giver,
Source of all that is and that shall be,
Mother and Father of us all,
Loving God, in whom is heaven:
The hallowing of your name echo
          through the universe!
The way of your justice be followed
          by the peoples of the world!
Your heavenly will be done by all
          created beings!
Your commonwealth of peace and
          freedom sustain our hope and come on earth.
With the bread we need for today, feed us.
In the hurts we absorb from one another, forgive us.
In times of temptation and test, strengthen us.
From trials too great to endure, spare us.
From the grip of all that is evil, free us.
For you reign in the glory of the power that is love,
now and forever. Amen.

The Blessing

The blessing of God,
the eternal goodwill of God,
the shalom of God,
the wildness and the warmth of God,
be among us and between us,
now and always. **Amen.**

The divine Spirit dwells in us.

Thanks be to God!

3

Jesus The Healer

It is no secret that for the last several years, there has been a renaissance of interest in the intersection of spirituality and science, specifically spirituality and healing. Authors such as Herbert Benson and Larry Dossey have published books, articles abound in all the major magazines, television specials explore new research, and important new studies are published, such as the Mid America Heart Study, published in the Archives of Internal Medicine last October, which demonstrated in a well done randomized, controlled, and blinded study using a group of over 1000 patients that prayer was associated with better outcomes following heart attack and cardiac surgery. At the same time, there has also been a renewed interest in researching the historical Jesus, evidenced just a week or two ago by an ABC Peter Jennings television news special about the historical life of this Jew from Nazareth, as well as countless books, documentaries, articles, and conferences. Because I share an interest in both of these areas, it seemed natural to find a way to fuse them, and see what we can discover about Jesus the Healer.

New Testament scholar Stevan Davies has written a book called "Jesus as Healer," and a statement he makes in the book can stand for the consensus of current study: "No fact about Jesus of Nazareth," he says, "is so widely and repeatedly attested in the gospels as the fact that he was a healer of people in mental and physical distress."

From my own study of the gospels, both canonical ones like Matthew, Mark, Luke, and John as well as non-canonical ones like the Gospel of Thomas, it seems clear to me that the person we call Jesus was a healer, and healing was central to his follower's ministry. My belief is that Jesus provides us with an image of healing the physical, mental, social, and spiritual dimensions of life that is very much akin to a modern, holistic view or model of bio-psycho-socio-spiritual illness and healing. For some moderns who engage in such healing, Jesus represents the theological foundation for their healing ministry. For others, of a wide variety of beliefs, he is a source of spiritual wisdom. I think there is much to be learned from using Jesus as an image of holistic healing, regardless of our faith or belief.

According to Christian scripture, Jesus heals many bodily ailments, including fever, paralysis, leprosy, blindness, deafness, a withered hand, excessive menstrual bleeding, edema, and other illnesses. Of course, it is not always possible to equate first or second-century descriptions with modern classifications of diseases. These healings of the body took place through words and touch. The rituals were simple, the words had no real magical quality to them, and occasionally an anointing took place, often with saliva and perhaps some dirt. The question we must ask ourselves is, how should we understand, from the words given us in ancient texts, the way in which Jesus' healing took place?

In his book, Davies says that if Jesus healed ailments such as the ones I've mentioned, then those cases were of a certain sort, not just any disorders but disorders of the kind that can be healed, on the spot, by the words or the self-presentation of the healer. He regards these disorders as psychosomatic in nature or, more precisely, as conversion disorders in which a person converts a psychological problem into a physical manifestation, something we call somatization disorder.

As Dr. Davies sees it, Jesus heals through the modality of forgiveness. He cites as a classic example of healing through forgiveness the story of the paralytic whose pallet is lowered through the roof into Jesus' presence, as told in the Gospel of Mark:

A few days later, when Jesus again entered Capernaum, the people heard that he had come home. So many gathered that there was no room left, not even outside the door, and he preached the word to them. Some men came, bringing to him a paralytic, carried by four of them. Since they could not get him to Jesus because of the crowd, they made an opening in the roof above Jesus and, after digging through it, lowered the mat the paralyzed man was lying on. When Jesus saw their faith, he said to the paralytic, "Son, your sins are forgiven." Now some teachers of the law were sitting there, thinking to themselves, "Why does this fellow talk like that? He's blaspheming! Who can forgive sins but God alone?" Immediately Jesus knew in his spirit that this was what they were thinking in their hearts, and he said to them, "Why are you thinking these things? Which is easier: to say to the paralytic, 'Your sins are forgiven,' or to say, 'Get up, take your mat and walk'? But that you may know that the Son of Man has authority on earth to forgive sins...." He said to the paralytic, "I tell you, get up, take your mat and go home." He got up, took his mat and walked out in full view of them all. This amazed everyone and they praised God, saying, "We have never seen anything like this!"

What are we to make of this explanation of Jesus' healings? On the one hand, the fact that this is the only story in Christian scripture linking forgiveness with healing of disease makes it a slim basis upon which to generalize about Jesus as a healer. On the other hand, conversion and somatization disorders must have occurred then as now. Just as Jesus addressed the issue of forgiveness with this man, which may have been the key to his cure, there is a role to be played today by a spiritual ministry that addresses guilt and forgiveness. Certainly the Roman Catholics think so in their sacraments of confession and absolution, and it is also a central feature of many 12-step programs such as Alcoholics Anonymous. Think about your own life for a moment. Have you ever felt healed by the act of releasing guilt or shame, or even by releasing it within yourself, or by asking another for their forgiveness? If healing is the central theme of Jesus' ministry, then unconditional forgiveness comes in a close second.

For Stevan Davies, forgiveness and faith healing will have a limited effect in cases of viral and bacterial infection. But he adds that if faith in a healer who promises forgiveness can immediately alleviate anxiety, stress, guilt, and so permit the full functioning of the somatic immune system, this may, in turn, help to eliminate diseases of viral or bacterial origins. As a chaplain, I have to ask myself if this doesn't suggest a wider role for clergy, pastoral counselors, and chaplains in the healing of physical illness.

I also have to ask myself about the power of prayer to heal, and it seems to me that this needs to be explained in two different ways. First, if the person who is experiencing the healing can hear my prayer, and my references to forgiveness, and therefore feels that forgiveness as a result of that prayer, then Davies hypothesis makes sense. But how do we explain randomized, controlled, double-blind, prospective, parallel-group studies like the one published last October in the Archives of Internal Medicine which demonstrated that intercessory prayer, or praying for others who were ill without their knowledge, was clearly associated with a better medical outcome in cardiac patients? More studies are obviously needed here, but this is about the third or fourth time this particular model has been replicated. At Grossmont Hospital, where I serve as chaplain, we will soon begin a similar 12-month study to see if there is any connection between pain control and prayer in orthopedic post-operative patients. Stay tuned.

Theologian and author Morton Kelsey takes a very different approach to understanding Jesus' healings. As he sees it, Jesus heals three kinds of illness: organic, functional, and mental. Most of Jesus' healings were of organic disease. Kelsey rejects attempts to explain Jesus' healings as relieving hysterical symptoms, though he does not deny that Jesus made some use of psychological methods. He characterizes Jesus' healing as the direct result of the healer's conscious and deliberate relationship to God. According to him, Jesus' methods did two things: they awakened the spirit that lay deep within these people, waiting to be touched. And at the same time his actions, words, and attitudes brought contact with the universal spirit, or the spirit of God. It would follow from Kelsey that one might engage in healing through words and touch, also known in sacrament as prayer and laying on of hands.

In modern medicine, one of the ways to act on the image of Jesus as healer is through a growing practice known as Healing Touch. Healing Touch certification workshops have sprung up all over the country, thousands of health care providers, especially nurses, have been certified, and many hospitals and hospices regularly offer it to their patients as an alternative medical practice in the relief of pain or other symptoms of illness. Author and healing touch practitioner Zach Thomas says that healing touch works through a process he calls hand-heart coordination, which he says is the human capacity to cooperate with God, or the universe, by communicating the heart's compassion through touch that facilitates the healing process. Unfortunately, he explains, touch has been subject to all kinds of abuses, and he has written of the periods in church history of healing touch, power touch, no touch, and touch gone wrong. When I train chaplains or talk to other ministers about touch, I find that the reactionary zealots of various denominations, including the UUA, have frightened many ministers and lay people into adopting a no touch approach out of sensitivity to its abuses, and as a result, we are robbing ourselves and others of the gift of human touch in appropriate and healing ways.

In a hospital environment, a chaplain or visitor can easily adopt a hands-off approach to spiritual presence, but my experience has taught me the importance of touching the person, be it a patient or our parishioner or our friend. Whether it is shaking hands, offering assistance to sit up in bed, holding hands as we talk or pray, or a simple touch to the shoulder or head for a greeting or as a blessing, touch is powerful medicine. Of course it is important to respect the person's preferences, ask permission, and employ proper infection control procedures when called for.

There is another dimension, another perspective if you will, of Jesus' healings that has not been written about much but which hospital chaplain Robert Richardson discusses in his recent article called "An Image of Holistic Care for the Sick," and that is the social implications of Jesus' healings. In the healing stories of the gospel, many portray the social situation of those who came for healing, demonstrating Jesus' attention to the poor and those who had no access to health care, to beggars, to widows, and to outcasts. These stories also differentiate Jesus from other healers who were his contemporaries.

The sick in Jesus' day were stigmatized and subject to social discrimination, conditions that we can relate to in our own time with the plagues of polio and AIDS. In his time and in ours, to put an end to this discrimination was an act of social criticism, which was an important part of Jesus' healing ministry. Social medicine has shown how unjust circumstances contribute to making people ill, so it is often impossible to heal the sick without healing their relationships, the circumstances in which they live, and the structures of the social system to which they belong.

The gospel of Mark is literally filled with stories of the social dimension of Jesus' healing. We have heard about the paralytic, unable to walk and dependent upon his litter bearers. There is the bricklayer with a withered hand, who would be handicapped from working. There is the possessed Gerasene man, a homeless person living among the tombs, a place of uncleanness and death. There is the woman with a hemorrhage, unclean as far as sexual relations are concerned and unclean religiously. And there is the leper, isolated from society and from religious participation, in chapter 1:

A man with leprosy came to him and begged him on his knees, "If you are willing, you can make me clean." Filled with compassion, Jesus reached out his hand and touched the man. "I am willing," he said. "Be clean!" Immediately the leprosy left him and he was cured. Jesus sent him away at once with a strong warning: "See that you don't tell this to anyone. But go, show yourself to the priest and offer the sacrifices that Moses commanded for your cleansing, as a testimony to them." Instead he went out and began to talk freely, spreading the news. As a result, Jesus could no longer enter a town openly but stayed outside in lonely places. Yet the people still came to him from everywhere.

These are the people to whom Jesus went or who approached him. Few would have access to physicians, and few were persons of power and authority. Jesus did not refuse healing to the rich and powerful, so he healed both the woman who had spent all her money on physicians and the daughter of the chief rabbi of the synagogue. Jesus healed across social and religious boundaries, and did not hesitate to touch those who the social structure of his day perceived to be unclean, whether due to hemorrhage, leprosy, or spirit. He touches the untouchables, and they are healed. He offers forgiveness, and the demons flee. But as the sad end of his story shows, physical and mental illness flee before him more readily than the domination systems of society and institutional religion. The more things change, it seems, the more they stay the same.

As a chaplain, I wonder what the social dimension of Jesus' healing means to me as we enter the twenty first century? If I could instantly restore physical and mental health, that would be wonderful. Or would it? Things were not always wonderful for Jesus or for those he healed. Then, as today, there is still the work of social healing to take place. I think I might encounter some opposition, just as Jesus did. In his day, some said, "You cannot heal on the Sabbath. It is against religious law." Some might say to me, "you cannot heal this person. It is against scientific law". And what of the bigger institutions, like drug companies, who only offer their healing touch to the highest bidder and use their power and influence to resist change in social structures that would clearly heal more people? This past week has seen alarming news come out of the International AIDS Conference in South Africa, where one out of every three teenage boys will not live to see twenty, and where access to the treatments of the West are denied for political and economic benefit?

Most kids in school know the story of Helen Keller, whose dark and silent world was finally penetrated by her teacher, Anne Sullivan. What many kids don't know about Keller is that she graduated from Radcliffe, became a radical socialist, and addressed the social causes of blindness in the exploitation of workers and of women. To follow the image of Jesus as healer today means to go beyond the miracle worker to the hard work of social healing.

So far, I haven't said much about faith, or spiritual healing. I know what spiritual care is, and I think I know what spiritual healing is, too. For me, spiritual care is helping someone use their faith, whatever that faith may be, in the service of their own healing. Spiritual healing is when wholeness is restored. When he healed, Jesus often finished with the words "go now, your faith had made you whole." Like any good hospital chaplain, he doesn't specify what faith that might be or require adherence to a doctrine or dogma before he offers healing to others. It is an unconditional gift.

Perhaps the most powerful gift we can give another is unconditional presence, unconditional acceptance, unconditional forgiveness, and unconditional love. Physical, mental, societal, and spiritual healing are available to us, and we can all affirm Jesus' example as a healer as a way to move toward those goals, regardless of our personal faith or belief.

4

A Ritual for Healing

The Ministry of the Word

Compassionate is our God,
Creator, Liberator, + and Comforter;

And blessed is Creation, now and forever. Amen.

A Reading from the Letter of James.

"Are any among you suffering? They should pray. Are any cheerful? They should sing songs of praise. Are any among you sick? They should call for the ministers of the church and have them pray over them, anointing them with oil in the name of God. The prayer of faith will save the sick, and our God will raise them up; and anyone who has strayed will be welcome and forgiven".

The Reconciliation

Hear God's word to all.
God shows love for us,
forgives us, welcomes us .

Amen.

If we confess our poor choices,
God is just, and may be trusted to forgive us
and cleanse and protect us from every kind of wrong.
In silence we call to mind our regrets and poor choices.

Let us confess our regrets.

**God of grace,
we confess that we have strayed
and made poor choices**

in what we have thought, and said, and done.
Forgive us and restore us to wholeness. Amen.

N., God forgives you. Forgive yourself, and know that
God pardons you and sets you free. **Amen.**

The Invocation

Like the first disciples before the coming of God's power
at Pentecost, we wait in faith, and pray.

(silence)

Be with us, Holy Wisdom;
nothing can separate us from your love.

Be with us as of old,

fill us with your power,
direct all our thoughts to your goodness.
Be present, Compassionate One;
bring faith and healing and peace.

(silence)

Our God is here.
God's Spirit is with us.

The Laying on of Hands and Anointing

N., in the name of God
I/we lay my/our hands upon you.
Receive God's healing touch to make you whole
in body, mind, and spirit.
The power of God strengthen you,
the love of God dwell in you
and give you peace. **Amen.**

(The healer dips a thumb in the holy oil and
makes the sign of the cross or medicine wheel on the
person's forehead, saying....)

N., I anoint you with this holy oil.
Receive God's forgiveness and healing.
The compassion of the Creator who loves you

flow through your mind and body and spirit,
lifting you to peace and inward strength.
Amen.

God our healer,
keep us aware of your presence,
support us with your power,
comfort us with your protection,
give us strength,
and establish us in your peace.

The Lord's Prayer

N., joining with those who pray for you and with the
whole church, we pray

**Our God in heaven, holy are your many names,
your kingdom come, your will be done, on earth
as in heaven. Give us today our daily bread, and
forgive us unconditionally even as we struggle to
give this same gift to others.
Save us from the times of trial, and deliver us from
evil. For the kingdom, and the power, and the
glory are yours now and forever. Amen.**

The Lord is my shepherd, therefore I lack nothing.
You make me lie down in green pastures,
and lead me beside the waters of peace.
You revive my spirit, and guide me in right pathways
for your name's sake.
Though I walk through the valley of the shadow of death,
I will fear nothing, for you are with me;
your rod and your staff are my comfort.
You spread a table for me in the sight of my enemies;
you have anointed my head with oil, and my cup
overflows. Surely your goodness and mercy shall follow
me all the days of my life, and I will dwell in the house of
God forever.

The Blessing

God be your comfort, your strength; God be your hope and support; God be your light and your way; and the blessing of God, +Creator, Liberator, and Giver of life, remain with you now and forever. **Amen.**

5

Table Fellowship for the 21ˢᵗ Century

First of all, let me be clear about what we are and are not doing today. My description of today's service in the newsletter was slightly misleading, as we won't be doing a "traditional" Universalist communion service. I actually think my thoughts on this have progressed even since I submitted that copy to Dolores for the newsletter. We will not be changing bread and juice into the body and blood of Jesus Christ, we will not be professing our faith in old-fashioned Christianity, and we will not be setting ourselves against the evils of Calvinism, as an old-time Universalist preacher might do. What we are going to do is talk about this person, and I stress the word person, called Jesus of Nazareth, re-imagine his life and message for spiritual seekers in the 21ˢᵗ century, and celebrate our one common humanity using a simple concept called table fellowship, which Jesus was a big fan of but which has been a part of most cultures and religions across time. Who we eat with, in Jesus time and in ours, says a lot about justice an inclusion in my view. I hope that I can get the inner meaning of that view across to all of you this morning.

First, as a way of totally stripping Jesus of his status as the Christ and making him completely human, I would like to share a reading from the UU pamphlet, "Unitarian Universalist Views of Jesus."

"Jesus or Joshua, son of Joseph, was born presumably in Nazareth of Galilee prior to 4 BCE. not in Bethlehem as Christmas stories imply. His mother's name was Mary or Miriam. He was a carpenter by trade as was his father before him. Evidently a person of high intelligence and sensitivity, he was attracted by the preaching of John the Baptist, and was baptized by him in the Jordan River.

"After John's arrest, Jesus broke with the Baptist Movement and began a preaching mission of his own. After John's execution, he became widely known in Galilee and Judea for his independent teaching and his ability to heal psychic and psychosomatic disorders. Because of his rather cavalier attitude toward the current rabbinical interpretation of the Torah, and especially toward the Sabbath regulations, the Jewish authorities arranged for his arrest in Jerusalem at the Passover Festival probably in 33 AD. Turned over to the Romans on a trumped up charge of insurrection, he was sentenced to death by crucifixion, and executed at Jerusalem. His teaching, apparently based on some profound personal experience, **rejected all outward religious forms** including baptism and Sabbath observance, and even tended to devalue specific ethical regulations. He taught that God loves all men and women indiscriminately, the evil as well and the good, and if we loved each other with the indiscriminate love of God, then that love would direct us to act ethically, would transmute evil to good, expunge sin and regenerate and in some sense deify the human soul."

I respond to this story by both affirming my faith as a liberal, progressive Christian and emphatically declaring my belief that Jesus did not ascend into heaven on the third day like the "space shuttle" in order to sit at the right hand of anybody, much less God, waiting for just the right moment to magically transport back to earth to set things right. He was a person; a prophet, a teacher, perhaps even a healer, but he was fully human and therefore everything he did and taught, we can do and teach, especially his unwavering Universalism. To talk about our own Universalist heritage is to tell you why I value the teachings of this Jesus enough to consider myself a Christian, and why Unitarian Universalism may be the last hope of saving the honest story of the progressive and liberal teachings left us by this Jew named Jesus.

In order to get to the heart of it, I don't think we can look seriously at the resurrection event as Unitarian Universalists without looking at UU views of who Jesus was, or even at what the faith of a liberal Christian might look like. Let's start there and take a look at what UU Minister Daniel Higgins has offered in words and images that describe his liberal Christian belief. He talks about mythology, and affirms that the informing myth of western culture is the Hebrew and Christian story. He says that this story is a vehicle of truth for him, and that concepts about what is right or wrong, views about the common good, family and societal responsibilities, all impact our culture and come from this one heritage. He is right, of course, and one of the primary reasons that I continue to frame my own religious faith through the Judeo-Christian story is because it is my heritage. Higgins sees God as creator; I see God as a process, not a person. He views scripture as a body of stories that describes the relationship of certain group of people in a certain slice of time with this God, and so contains usable guidelines on living one's life. He does not describe Jesus' divinity but does describe his teachings, which is a common way for UUs to be in fellowship with Jesus, I think. Let me share some of his words:

"Jesus' teachings, particularly the parables, are illustrative of a spirit in which life is to be lived. They are not laws but principles, exemplifying patience, mercy, forgiveness, self-control, and good will. When asked which is the greatest commandment, Jesus answered: "You shall love your God with all your heart, with all your soul, and with all your mind, and with all your strength, and you shall love your neighbor as yourself." He not only restated the Jewish prayer expressing faith in love of God, he universalized it, and he lived it. In a profound and tragic way his message and life were one. His broad sympathies, his ministry to the sick and outcast, his affection for the poor and despised brought down upon him the crushing retribution of civil and religious authorities."

Most of the UU Christians I have read seem to begin with the humanity of Jesus, which is the same humanity in all people, and accept the divinity in Jesus (known in his divinity as the Christ) only insofar as it says something about the potential of universal human nature, meaning that the divinity in Jesus points to the divinity in all persons. Some assert that whatever is true about Jesus is true about each of us in general, at least potentially, and that this is basic to any UU understanding of the incarnation or divinity of Christ. To quote 19th Century British Unitarian James Martineau, "The incarnation is true, not of Christ exclusively, but of humanity universally."

This has certainly always squared with my own vision of Jesus, and others who followed him like Ghandi or Martin Luther King. Hindus believe that God is incarnate in various religious leaders throughout history. God is not revealed in one person and one place in history only, but in many persons and in various places throughout history. My own spiritual anchor has to be that the divine spirit isn't just potentially present but is present in all living beings.

As Unitarian Universalists, I know that we get hung up with words like "God" or "divinity". So re-imagine them. Change them to whatever works for you, because in the end we are all talking about the same thing. I know I have preached about religious history and writings as myth before. I guess the real question we should ask ourselves is, what is a myth, and what do they mean for us? Every civilization, every culture, every religion has a mythology made up of stories and legends that inform faith and practice. They nourish and build community, aid us all in our search for meaning, and ask the big questions: Who am I? What is the meaning of life? Can I know ultimate reality? What new myths must we write and live out in community that can help us all make meaning of this incredibly small slice of time we are given to be alive in our universe?

My favorite collection of Christian myths is the Gospel of John. I like to imagine myself as a character in some of its stories, and I like it because in addition to breaking bread with his disciples at that last meal together, Jesus washes their feet as an ultimate symbol of love and service and humanity. I like to imagine myself sitting in a darkened room, surrounded by my closest friends, sharing a meal together in a time when that simple act, who you ate with and where you ate, spoke volumes about your status, your willingness to be inclusive, even your integrity. That is the real power of the table fellowship that Jesus taught and that we will reenact in just a few minutes. In their rush to dominate their followers and read every biblical passage literally, the fundamentalists seem to forget that Jesus declared poor people and tax collectors and prostitutes and the marginalized and all manner of sinners forever welcome at God's table by making the choices he made about whom to share his table with. Jesus would have appreciated the concept of a "welcoming Congregation", I think.

The liberal, progressive lens through which we view these old stories reminds us that we are forever welcome at the table, forever a special and unrepeatable part of creation. That is the essence of our traditional Universalism, and the simple act of sharing bread and wine together is the ritual that Jesus and many before him left for us to continually reaffirm our precious contribution to the cycles of our universe, and to remind us that we cannot be one body until we exclude no one from our table, from our society. As we stand together this morning in our closing circle, we will pass to each other a plate of bread and a glass of juice to dip that bread into, a practice our Christian friends call communion by intinction. Let us do that not as Christians or even theists, but as a symbol of our community and our inclusiveness and our joy at being born into such a magical universe.

Most mainstream Christians today seem so engrossed in the birth and death stories of Jesus that they forget what happened in between, and it is here that our liberal Universalism can offer a corrective. While those Christians may find a sincere religious experience in their belief in the divine risen Christ, I find an equally sincere belief in the human Jesus who gave himself, totally, to the divinity that is in each of us. As we walk under the skies of yet another miraculous spring, I'd like to end with a prayer from our own UU Hymnal:

"Oh Spirit of life and renewal, we have wintered enough, mourned enough, oppressed ourselves enough. Our souls are too long cold and buried, our dreams all but forgotten, and our hopes unheard. We are waiting to rise from the dead. In this, the season of steady rebirth, we awaken to the power so abundant, so holy, that returns each year through earth and sky. We will find our hearts again in our good spirits. We will love and believe and give and wonder and feel again the eternal powers. The flow of life moves ever onward through one faithful spring and another and now another. May we be forever grateful."

6

A Ritual for Table Fellowship

❖

(an inclusive communion)

Hymn or other Opening Music

A Bell is rung
The Invocation

> In the name of our Creator who shares divinity
> with us; our brother Jesus who shares humanity with us;
> the Spirit who unsettles and inspires us;
> let us give thanks.

> **Glory to God forever and ever.**

> We declare this space and our time together to be holy.
> Enter God's gates with thanksgiving and come to the
> table with praise.

> **Glory be to God most High.**

> Let us pray.

(A prayer, collect, or meditation may be said)

A Bell is rung

The Reconciliation

> Hear God's word to all.
> God shows love for us,
> forgives us, welcomes us.

Listen to our hearts, loving God.

If we confess our poor choices,
God is just, and may be trusted to forgive us
and cleanse and protect us from every kind of wrong.
In silence we call to mind our regrets and poor choices.

(silence)

**God of grace,
we confess that we have strayed and made poor
choices in what we have thought, and said, and done.
Forgive us and restore us to wholeness.**

God forgives you.
Forgive yourself, and know that God
pardons you and sets you free.

A Bell is rung

The Readings

*Readings from world scripture and other sources may be
included here. At the beginning of each reading, the
reader should say: "Listen to what the spirit is saying to
her people. A reading from...."*

*Music, sung psalms, drumming, dance or movement are
all appropriate here.*

Homily/Meditation/Sharing

*This is an informal meditation and discussion on the
readings as well as the feelings they evoke in the
participants. A bell or talking stick may be used to claim
individual sacred space, and passed from person to
person. You may speak or remain silent, in the Quaker
tradition, as you wish.*

A Liturgical Affirmation

A Bell is rung

Let us share our vision for healing and wholeness.

I believe in a Higher Power; God, Creator, Mother, Father, Lover, Friend, who is love and who has given the earth to all living things.

I believe in Jesus of Nazareth, who came to heal us and to free us from all forms of oppression. I believe he taught us to:

* Love each other, and love ourselves.
* Live authentically, with rigorous honesty and
	integrity.
* Help and defend those who cannot help and defend
	themselves.
* Heal, visit, and feed.
* Accept no violence.
* Be a witness for tolerance and inclusion for all
	people.
* Above all, forgive.

These things are what it means to be a Christian, and I honor as saints those men and women who have given me examples to follow.

I believe in the Great Spirit, deliverer of grace, who works in and through all who have turned towards the truth. I believe in the community of faith that is called to be at the service of all people.

I believe in Jesus' promise to finally destroy the power of greed and selfishness in us all, and to establish the kingdom of equality, justice, and peace to all creation.

Exchange of the Peace

Blessed be Jesus, the Prince of Peace.
Who breaks down the walls that divide.

The peace of God be always with you!
And also with you!

*Announcements, special celebrations, music or performance
pieces are all appropriate here. The gathering may greet each
other in peace. Offerings and gifts of food or clothing may
be accepted here.*

The Prayers and Table Fellowship

The Creator is here.
God's Spirit is with us.

Lift your hearts to Creation.
Where Jesus proclaims justice for all.

Let us give thanks to God.
It is right to offer thanks and praise.

All glory to you, Giver of Life,
sufficient and full for all creation.
Accept our praises, living God,
for Jesus the Liberator, as radical in his time
as we are in ours, who on his last night
with his friends shared bread and wine,
your gifts from the earth.
He blessed them and reminded his
closest friends to remember him and his
ministry of love and justice each time
they came together to break bread
and share the cup.

Therefore we join in the chorus of praise
that rings throughout eternity, with
angels and archangels, prophets and martyrs,
creatures of earth, sea, and sky and all the holy women
and men of every age and culture.
Together with rocks, hills, waters,
mountains, suns and stars,
we co-create you as we say/sing:

**Holy, holy, holy,
God of love, giver of life;
earth and sea and sky**

**and all that lives,
declare your presence and your glory.**

A Bell is rung

> *As the bread is broken:* **Breaking bread
> symbolizes our willingness to welcome
> everyone to our table; to offer love and
> reconciliation to all, and to share our divinity
> as an unconditional gift.**

> *As the cup is lifted:* **Sharing this cup symbolizes
> our participation in Jesus' community
> practice of solidarity, justice-making,
> and love for our friends.**

> Let us put before God our prayers for ourselves,
> each other, our community, and the world.

A Bell is rung
Prayers may be offered silently or aloud.
Participants may light candles of concern.

> Come, Holy Wisdom, come. Gather the breath
> of life from all who are present here, and
> combine this essence with your blessing to
> make these gifts for us the symbolic presence
> of the Christ Spirit. Pour out your love upon the
> whole universe, and make us your new
> creation. In the fullness of time, bring us,
> with {   and} all your saintly people,
> from every tribe and language and people and
> nation, to feast at the table prepared deep in the
> promised land of peace. **Amen.**

A Bell is rung

> And now, joining with those who pray for
> us and with the whole community, we say:

> **Earth-maker, Pain-bearer, Life-giver,
> Source of all that is and that shall be,**

Mother and Father of us all,
Loving God, in whom is heaven:

The hallowing of your name echo through the
universe! The way of your justice be followed by the
peoples of the world! Your heavenly will be done by
all created beings! Your commonwealth of peace and
freedom sustain our hope and come on earth.

With the bread we need for today, feed us.
In the hurts we absorb from one another,
forgive us. In times of temptation and test,
strengthen us. From trials too great to endure,
spare us. From the grip of all that is evil, free us.
For you reign in the glory of the power that is
love, now and forever. Amen.

The elements are prepared and held up.

The gifts of God for the people of God.

The bread and wine are shared by saying
"N, This is the bread of life. Take it and be bread for the world."
"N, This is the cup of compassion. Drink it and be filled with grace."

During communion, music or drumming is appropriate,
as is a time of silent meditation and prayer.

The People's Response

A Bell is rung.

Let us be in prayer together.

Holy are you, God of all Creation,
for you have given us a meal
to celebrate community one with another.
May we who eat this bread be
servants to those in need,
may we who drink this cup
testify to the wonder of Creation.
May we delight in our bodies and minds,

**calling others into joy and life and wholeness.
Give us the opportunity to take
these gifts to our neighbors,
courage to speak truth and build community,
and wisdom to enjoy our eternal gifts. Amen.**

Closing Prayers and Dismissal

Listen to the words of the Sioux:
Great Spirit, All over the world the faces of living ones
are alike. With tenderness they have come
up out of the ground. Look upon your children
that they may face the winds and walk the good
road to the Day of Quiet.

Great Spirit, Fill us with the light.
Give us the strength to understand,
and the eyes to see.
Teach us to walk the soft earth
as relatives to all that live.

Shalom, So Be It, Amen.

Friends, continue your journey, walking in love.
Care for one another, care for the earth.
Seek justice and make peace.
May God's holy, healing, enabling Spirit
be with you every step of the way,
and may the blessing of God our
Creator, Liberator, and Giver of life
be with you and among you
now and forever. **Amen.**

My sisters and brothers,
go in peace to love and serve Creation.

Thanks be to God. Alleluia, Alleluia!

7

On Being a Minister

I want to begin this morning with an apology. Sometimes I just can't hide how irreverent I really am. I wanted to keep this sermon fairly serious, and some of it will be, but I just can't talk about being a minister unless I tell some priest, rabbi, and minister jokes.

So a priest, a rabbi and a minister were all in a boat out in the middle of a lake. The Minister says, "I am thirsty. I will go to shore and get something to drink." So he gets out of the boat walks across the water to shore, gets a soda, walks back across the water, and gets back in the boat. The Priest says, "I am thirsty also. I will go to shore and get something to drink." So he gets out of the boat walks across the water to shore, gets a soda, walks back across the water, and gets back in the boat. The rabbi thinks to himself "pretty cool. I will try it." So he says, "I am thirsty also. I will go to shore and get something to drink." He gets out of the boat and falls in the water and drowns. Then the priest said to the minister, "Do you think we should have told him where the rocks were?"

One day, a minister, a priest and a rabbi went for a hike. It was very hot. They were sweating and exhausted when they came upon a small lake. Since it was fairly secluded, they took off all their clothes and jumped in the water. Feeling refreshed, the trio decided to pick a few berries while enjoying their "freedom." As they were crossing an open area, who should come along but a group of ladies from town. Unable to get to their clothes in time, the minister and the priest covered their privates and the rabbi covered his face while they ran for cover. After the ladies had left and the men got their clothes back on, the minister and the priest asked the rabbi why he covered his face rather than his privates. The rabbi replied, "I don't know about you, but in MY congregation, it's my face they would recognize.

This morning I want to talk about what it means to me to be a minister, or a priest or a rabbi or a clergyperson or whatever name you want to call it. I want to talk about what it means to me, about what I think it means to my friends who are clergy, about what it means to society in general, and about what I think it means to you as a quirky but otherwise pretty normal Unitarian Universalist congregation. We are going to talk about the mystery of "call", how ministers are treated, what drives them to do what they do, how clergy roles sometimes differ, and I hope that my comments spark a lively exchange during our circle discussion. If nothing else, we can share each other's priest, rabbi, and minister jokes.

Virtually every people, culture, and belief system across all of human history have set aside men and women to celebrate the cycles of the universe and point out the sacred in everyday life. Often these people have been healers, and sometimes they have been people who could see into the future. They have often been though of as people with special gifts, and in some traditions they have been required to endure unnatural and even torturous requirements and lifestyles in order to prove their worth and call. In our own American culture, these people were first recognized as white male protestant ministers, especially Unitarians and Universalists, and our county's history books are filled with such examples as Ralph Waldo Emerson or William Ellery Channing. In our day, we have begun to embrace our theological diversity, and eastern, western, and native cultures and religions work together side by side on issues of peace and justice and human rights and many, many others, typically led by their clergy or religious professionals.

My Harper-Collins Dictionary of Religion lumps all of these historical manifestations under the term "priesthood", priest being from the Greek presbuteros, which means elder. This dictionary defines priests and priestesses as "holy persons by virtue of professional office; individuals, often belonging to a hereditary caste and usually male, who are formally inducted into the service of god or the gods in a holy place."

The lives and work of these various clergy are often veiled in mystery and tradition, and as a result we have tended to continue to think of clergy as apart from us in some way. I know this just in my own life and experience; imagine the response, having a first date over coffee, when I tell my date that I'm a minister. Instantly, every image that person has of clergy, every bad experience with institutional religion, every projection of privilege, everything their family ever taught them about ministers or priests or rabbis come crashing into their head. I know this when they choke on their beverage and say with a curious change in the tone of their voice "oh isn't that interesting". Sometimes I play with this and tell people I'm a social worker. I never get the same kind of response. When people find out that I'm a minister, they immediately put their guard up and assume that I will be shocked by or disapproving of ordinary human behavior. In their concern that I will judge them, they end up judging me. Even friends and co-workers have certain expectations of me because they know I'm a minister.

While I can appreciate a good clergy joke as well as the next guy, I also know how much our culture is shaped by literature and the media. Members of my profession are usually portrayed in one of three ways; the stupid, wimpish, pathetic minister who is regarded as a joke, the intellectual and wise but cloistered person who is completely out of touch with culture and reality; or maybe the self-righteous, authoritarian person who gets caught somewhere with his pants down.

In reality, the expectations that people have of religious professionals are huge. We are called to be expert theologians, scholars of world scripture, ethicists, counselors, therapists, administrators, and educators, facilitators of groups, liturgists, preachers, church historians, philosophers, and community organizers. Then for good measure throw in party planners and fundraisers. But being a minister gets even more complicated. Many professions require extensive preparation but few overlay powerful pressure on their members to be "special" people——people who are "icons" of morality, who are never in doubt or confused about life, who cope with everything and everybody with peaceful competence. And I'm sure we are the only profession who, through the ordination process, is forced to prove to some committee our very worth as human beings before we are allowed to even apply for a job.

I'm not saying this life we clergy live is a burden, obviously we all choose it out of some strong call and commitment, but I am asking you to put yourself in this place the next time you hold your minister or any other clergy person up to a higher standard than you'd hold your next-door neighbor who's a plumber. When you do that to a minister you rob him or her of their humanity. I want to stay with that thought for a few minutes and talk specifically about how Unitarian Universalist congregations do this.

A minister friend of mine has been in the search process here in southern California for the last few months, and has been on some interviews as well as gone through guest preaching in a neutral pulpit while search committees looked on. In one experience of preaching and then interviewing, she encountered a member of the search committee who openly stated that he didn't like ministers and though that the UU movement could do without them. This guy is on a SEARCH COMMITTEE. Can you imagine how this must make potential candidates feel? Imagine going on a job interview where a member of the interview panel thinks your position should be eliminated and makes that clear to you. And this story is by no means isolated; I meet with my San Diego County clergy colleagues every other month, and part of our time together is a relaxed check-in. Never have I attended a meeting where someone didn't have some story of emotional and sometimes physical abuse on the part of a church member. It is epidemic, and virtually unspoken of, typically out of fear.

It is my own personal experience that no denomination treats its clergy with quite as much distain as Unitarian Universalists. I think there are many reasons for this, but the one I think is most applicable is we are a movement of refugees. Many of you have come from other faiths, and perhaps have had bad experiences of institutional religion. Ministers tend to represent such institutions. Many humanists have difficulty setting someone apart as a religious professional. I suppose there are many other reasons too, and I don't mean to hand all the blame to you. Those of us who are clergy do two very important things very badly; we do not tell you the truth, and we do not maintain our boundaries.

When you have taken up countless minutes in a committee meeting making the same point over and over again we do not politely ask you to stop. When you interrupt our private lives with something that seems important to you but isn't important to us we don't tell you to call back at a better time. Few people are called to live their private lives within their public professions. When you treat us with passive-aggression we do not confront you. We freely come into the office to meet with you on our days off and will cancel a vacation half way around the world to return for an unexpected event in the life of the fellowship.

I live out my call to the ministry as a hospital chaplain, as many of you know. You also may know that I enjoy visiting with you and guest preaching, and I hope that you'll ask me back even after today. But I know, deep inside my heart, that I do not have what it takes to be a parish minister. My gifts and skills are well suited to pastoral care, and I hold in high regard those people who can sustain a successful career as a parish clergyperson. Its funny because my clergy friends always tell me how they could never be a chaplain, the stress is just too high. But I love my job because I have challenging responsibilities, enjoy the respect of my colleagues and peers, am paid as a professional with graduate school preparation, and am consistently appreciated by the people I serve. Many, many parish ministers cannot make these claims, and that makes me sad.

Now, I have been using strong words and images and so I think a disclaimer is called for, and then maybe another minister joke. The disclaimer is that no one has asked me to stand before you today and beat up on how UU congregations treat their ministers. Furthermore, this fellowship has no reputation anywhere for treating its clergy badly, as near as I can tell and I can say that out of personal experience. You are not without your cute little quirks but then again neither am

I. The issues I speak of today exist in every single denominational structure and in every religious institution in America. My message is meant to make a whole movement think a little harder before it treats it's clergy as something other than fallible, fragile, wonderful creations of God.

OK so this guy was sitting inside his local pub one day, enjoying a quiet beer and generally feeling good about himself, when a nun suddenly appears at his table and starts giving him a hard time about drinking. "You should be ashamed of yourself young man! Drinking is a Sin! Alcohol is the blood of the devil!" Now the gets pretty annoyed about this, and goes on the offensive. "How do *you* know, Sister?" "My Mother Superior told me so." "The guy says but have you ever had a drink yourself? How can you be sure that what you are saying is right?" The nun says Don't be ridiculous—of course I have never taken alcohol myself" "Then let me buy you a drink, says the guy, if you still believe afterwards that it is evil I will give up drinking for life" "How could I, a Nun, sit next to you drinking?!" "The guy thinks about it and says I'll get the barman to put it in a teacup for you, them no-one will know" The Nun reluctantly agrees, so the guy walks over to the bartender. "Another beer for me, and a triple vodka on the rocks", then he lowers his voice and says to the bartender "…and could you put the vodka in a teacup?" The bartender looks at him and says "Oh no! It's not that drunken Nun again is it?"

By now you are probably asking, why do people become clergy if they get treated as badly as Don says? For many of us, it really is a difficult-to explain call, or pull, or even just an intuitive sense that we are meant to follow this path. Ancient indigenous religions chose the ones they thought were different or set apart, but in our time we have to discern that within ourselves. I knew I was meant to be a hospital chaplain when I began working with early AIDS patients in the late eighties. It was as clear as day, no discernment required. I get to help people make meaning out of the most meaningful events of their lives. I had a chance to see the Broadway version of The Lion King a few weeks ago, and the character I always identify with most is Rafiki, the medicine man or shaman. The actor who plays Rafiki is a woman, which I think is particularly appropriate. Rafiki is a storyteller, a keeper of the traditions, a healer who stays off to the side and out of the limelight but is always there when needed somehow and is never afraid to take a stand or lead the way when necessary. To say that I became a minister because I want to help people seems too simple. I became a minister because I knew I had to and now I can't imagine being anything else. That is where we share a common humanity, you and I. When you discover what you are meant to do in the world you just know it, don't you? And isn't it the most wonderful thing ever?

I guess that is my point this morning. That we share humanity equally regardless of what we are called to do in the world. Whenever you treat someone differently just because of what they are called to do, you somehow diminish their humanity. In Hebrew scripture, when the people of Israel were waiting on the banks of the Jordan River to enter the promised land, God told Joshua to tell the priests: 'lift up the ark of the covenant and pass in front of the people. Tell them that when they come to the edge of the waters of the Jordan, they are to take their stand in the river".

Well I have a better image, of us all inviting each other to take our stand in the river, and of watching for the ones among us who will take hold of the dream and show us how they stepped into the river of life, the ones who will tell us what it feels like in the river, and the ones who will demonstrate what we need to carry with us if we are to live in that river with faith, integrity, and a sense of adventure. That's what I think clergy are supposed to do, and I am humbled and blessed to be able to do it.

8

Ordination and Commissioning for Ministry

The Gathering

Prelude

Processional Hymn (if desired)

Glory to God, Creator, Redeemer, and Giver of Life
who is, who was, and is to come.
Grace and Peace to you from God.

God fill you with truth and joy.

Reconciliation (appropriate words may be chosen)

The Universe loves us and forgives us.
Forgive others, forgive yourself.

The Presentation

Poetry or Anthem

People of God, we have come to ordain
(or commission) a (   )in God's
servant community. God calls us to and is the source
of our ministry. We stand within a tradition in which
there are spiritual leaders and teachers who
are called and empowered to fulfill an ordained
(or commissioned) ministry and to enable the whole
mission of the Thomas Christians.

Our authority is in scripture, the teachings of Jesus of
Nazareth, the Gospel of Thomas, and in the Church's

continuing practice, reason, and experience through the
ages. Therefore let us welcome N (s), now
presented to us, to be ordained (commissioned)
as (   ).

Each candidate is presented by a person or
persons of their choosing.

> **Bishop N.,we present N., who has been chosen**
> **by the Thomas Christian community, to be**
> **a (   ) in the Church. We believe that**
> **he/she will serve God and Creation.**
>
> N., do you believe that you are called to the
> office and work of a (   )?
>
> <u>Each Candidate</u>: **I believe that God and the Church are**
> **calling me to this ministry. I thank God for this call,**
> **and my brother and sister clergy for their**
> **encouragement.**
>
> People of God, are you willing that N. should be
> ordained?
>
> **We are. Thanks be to God.**
>
> Let us pray.
> Holy and Living God, you call women and men to bring
> to us your creative and redeeming presence.
> Equip your people for their work of ministry
> and give to this/these your servant(s), now to be ordained,
> the gifts of grace s/he (they) need (s). **Amen.**

The Proclamation of the Word

> The Readings:
> *(Appropriate readings are chosen. At least one should*
> *be from the Gospel of Thomas).*
>
> Sermon:
> *(Usually, the ordaining convener/bishop)*
>
> Statement of Faith:
> *(Chosen, written, and read by the candidates)*

The Commitment

N, you have declared your faith in God.
We believe God is calling you to serve.
We now ask you to declare again your
commitment to our fellowship.

Will you work wholly for the true benefit of God's
Holy Community, continuing with care the office
committed to you, refraining from using the power for
your own ends?

I will, with the help of God.

Do you believe that the scriptures of the world
and the Gospel of Thomas contain all that is
essential for right relationship, and reveal God's
living word?

**Yes, I do. God give me understanding in studying
world scripture. May they reveal to me your mind
and heart, and shape my ministry.**

Will you be constant in prayer and study?

I will. God give me imagination and perseverance.

Will you accept the order and discipline of this Church
and the guidance and leadership of your mentors?

**Yes, I will. God give me grace to work in partnership
with my sisters and brothers in God's service.**

Will you join with God's people in seeking the lost and
lonely, in healing the sick and ministering to all,
whatever their needs? Will you live the gospels
in faith, and challenge us with the demands of love?

**I will. My concern will be to show love and
compassion. God give me courage to strive for justice,
wholeness, and peace among all people. I commit
myself fully to this ministry.**

Will you pray faithfully and expectantly, alone
and with the whole Community?

**Yes, I will. Prayer will inspire my ministry. I will
constantly seek the mind of God and
celebrate God's presence with joy.**

(*Individually to each candidate*)

Finally, do you, N., here and now affirm your lifelong
commitment to the Thomas Christian community?

I do. Thanks be to God.

The Invocation and Ordination

Interlude (*music, poetry, other ritual expression*)

Like the first disciples waiting for your coming,
empowering Spirit, we wait in faith and pray.

Silence

Great Spirit of God, meet us in this moment
as you met the apostles of old. Be with us, Great Spirit.

**Bring faith and hope, we pray.
Come, Healer Spirit.
Be present in your power.**

(*The Candidate(s) moves before the bishop and kneels*)

Holy are you, God our creator, God in history, God
revealed; throughout the ages your unchanging love
has created a people to love and serve the cosmos.
Blessed are you, in Jesus of Nazareth,
whose teachings are a great gift and whose ministry of
love we follow in joy. We thank you for calling this your
servant N. to share in this great work of love and
compassion.

(*All present lay hands on each candidate individually*)

**God of grace, through your Holy Spirit,
gentle as a dove, living, burning as fire,
empower your servant N. for the office and work of a
(   ) in the Church.**

May every grace of ministry rest on this your
servant. Keep her/him faithful and strong,
and may s/he point us to love and justice in Jesus.

**Amen! May s/he point us to God, the
living way, and unite us in love, rejoicing!**

The Celebrant gives the Gospel of Thomas, saying

N, here are the teachings of Jesus.
Learn from them, teach them, live by them,
and proclaim Christ, the living Word.

9

Ethics for the New Millennium

I would like to begin my remarks this morning by reading a paragraph or two from the Preface of a book called "Ethics for the New Millennium", written by His Holiness The Dalai Lama:

Having lost my country at the age of sixteen and become a refugee at twenty-four, I have faced a great many difficulties during the course of my life. When I consider these, I see that a lot of them were insurmountable. Not only were they unavoidable, they were incapable of favorable resolution. Nonetheless, in terms of my own peace of mind and physical health, I can claim to have coped reasonably well. As a result, I have been able to meet adversity with all my resources—-mental, physical, and spiritual. I could not have done so otherwise. Had I been overwhelmed by anxiety and despaired, my health would have been harmed. I would also have been constrained in my actions.

Looking around, I see that it is not only we Tibetan refugees, and members of other displaced communities, who face difficulties. Everywhere and in every society, people endure suffering and adversity—even those who enjoy freedom and material prosperity. Indeed, it seems to me that much of the unhappiness we humans endure is actually of our own making. In principle, therefore, this is at least avoidable. I also see that, in general, those individuals whose conduct is ethically positive are happier and more satisfied than those who neglect ethics. This confirms my belief that if we can reorientate our thoughts and emotions, and reorder our behavior, not only can we learn to cope with suffering more easily, but we can prevent a great deal of it from arising in the first place.

My hope this morning is to take this wonderful, broad-brush theme of Ethics for a New Millennium and do several things in an always too brief period of time. First, I'd like to define ethics so we all know what we're talking about, and I want to look at some contemporary ethical systems, theories, and problems. I'd like to see if there is something in our liberal religious voice that we can contribute to the national dialogue about ethics in many disciplines, and then see what such an ethic might mean for us religious liberals. Finally, I want to draw upon the wisdom of the Dalai Lama, and Buddhist tradition in general, to frame my remarks and our discussion later this morning.

This past Friday, as I was frantically trying to write this sermon in between phone calls and all manner of crises at the hospital, I was challenged by two different ethical dilemmas even before lunch. Medical Ethics is but one small branch in the whole discipline of ethics, which is mostly the realm of philosophers and theologians. But at the bedside, doctors, nurses and even chaplains are called upon to become moral and philosophical decision makers, especially when patients can't speak for themselves. In one of my cases, I looked into the wide-open eyes of a thirty-year-old woman, profoundly retarded and unable to communicate with end-stage muscular dystrophy, multiple infections, and respiratory failure, and recommended to her physicians that they withdraw life support. I did this confident of my intellectual position, that of the futility of anything medicine had to offer her combined with the below minimal level of her quality of life, and I made this recommendation from my head while my heart hurt for her and her situation. A Hispanic woman, essentially dumped at the border when her family could no longer care for her, she has been shuffled from institution to institution without any family or friends around her, perhaps without even knowing where she was or how she got there. One of the duties of the discipline of ethics is to help us to decide what is right and moral in such difficult cases.

My paperback, second college edition of The American Heritage Dictionary defines ethics as "principles of right or good conduct or a body of such principles". Additional definitions given include "a system of moral principles or values" and "the study of the general nature of morals and of specific moral choices." I then sped ahead to page 444 and looked up "moral", and found that morals are concerned with the discernment or instruction of what is good and evil, and is also used in the context of being or acting in accordance with established standards of good behavior, or even rules or habits of conduct. In the case of medical ethics, the system of moral principles we bring to bear includes ancient wisdom from the Hippocratic oath, reminding healers of their duty to assist those in need as well as to do no harm.

We also look at the ethical principle of autonomy, or the right of each individual to make their own choices where such choices do no harm to others. When an individual cannot exercise their right of autonomy, as was the case with my Hispanic patient last Friday, then others must consider the ethical principle of quality of life. In all these considerations, it is considered ethical and appropriate to also consider contextual factors like culture and religion, and in the case of limited resources such as organ donations, we must also examine the ethical principle of distributive justice, meaning the fair and equitable distribution of burdens and benefits within a community. But as I said earlier, medical ethics is just one small part of the overall discipline of ethics. There is business ethics, organizational ethics, professional ethics, and various codes of ethics. It seems that our society has embraced the notion of ethics as the best way to order behavior and relations, especially when trying to legislate such matters seems inappropriate or unworkable.

In my view, two very helpful contributions to the ethics of human interaction and behavior have come from ethical thinkers decades apart, the first from an Episcopal priest and the second from a Dalai Lama. The first, written some time ago by Joseph Fletcher, is called "Situation Ethics; The New Morality". In it, Father Fletcher asserts that that there are really only three approaches to follow in making moral decisions: the legalistic, or the notion that every decision-making situation that one enters into is resolved through the use of prefabricated rules and regulations, in not just the spirit but the letter of the law. The second approach is the polar opposite of legalistic, where one enters into a decision-making situation armed with no principles or community standards whatsoever, to say nothing of rules. In every unique situation, this theory holds, one must rely upon the situation of itself, then and there, to provide its ethical solution.

The third way, and the one advocated by Fletcher throughout his book, is situationism or situation ethics. In this approach, the situationist enters into every decision-making opportunity fully armed with the rules and ethical maxims of his or her community and its heritage, and they are treated with respect as illuminators or guides about how to think about the problem. But just the same, the situationist is prepared in any situation to compromise those rules or set them aside in the situation if love seems better served by doing so. Situation Ethics, in other words, is doing what love requires.

Fletcher likes to tell the story of the rich married man who asked a lovely young woman he had just met at a bar if she would sleep the night with him. She, of course, said no. He then asked if she would do it for $100,000. and she said yes! He then asked if she would do it for $10,000. and she replied, "well, yes." Finally, he asked "how about $500." In a very insulted tone, the woman replied 'what do you think I am?" and the rich man answered, "We have already established **that**. Now we are haggling over the price" He uses this story to ask if such situations as marital infidelity or taking money for sex always lead to a conclusion of immoral behavior in every single circumstance, or might the conclusion be different in different circumstances?

Writing much more recently than Fletcher, in fact just last year, His Holiness The Dalai Lama published a book, the title of which I plagiarized for the title of this sermon today. In it, he focuses on the very Buddhist notion of inner peace as he discusses first the foundation of ethics, then ethics and the individual, and finally ethics and society as a whole.

For the Dalai Lama, the foundation of ethics is, to use his term, "positive ethical conduct." For him, the core of human conduct is all about the quest for human happiness. He makes the observation that everywhere, by all means imaginable, people are striving to improve their lives. Yet his impression is that those living in materially developed countries, for all their industry, are in some ways less satisfied, less happy, and to some extent suffer more than those living in the least developed countries. He worries that those with more material things are so caught up with the idea of acquiring still more that they make no room for anything else in their lives. As a hospital chaplain, I wonder if this isn't true in the quest of some people to continue to want to keep their loved ones alive, or to continue to insist upon treatments for themselves or others long after those treatments would be helpful, no matter what the cost or quality of life. Those in under developed countries have no such decisions to make, because advanced medicine isn't available to them.

In consideration of a foundational ethical statement, the Dalai Lama offers this: that an ethical act is one that does not harm others' experience or expectation of happiness. He discusses the importance of taking others' feelings into consideration, and of ideals such as restraint, virtue, and compassion. He does not claim that suffering has a purpose, and he places it with equal footing in the circle of life, or in the cycles of the seasons and the universe. He encourages time spent in discernment, and claims that society has certain universal responsibilities, as well as levels of commitment to those responsibilities.

Both of these ethical systems, the situation ethics of Joseph Fletcher and the Buddhist ethics of the Dalai Lama are present in the community norms, or ethics, of virtually every liberal religious movement, and I guess that must be why I find a home in this movement. The covenant of the Unitarian Universalist Association, and the creeds and covenants of many liberal religious organizations, call us to such high ideals as affirming and promoting the inherent worth and dignity of every person; justice, equity, and compassion in human relations; acceptance of one another, which certainly implies tolerance, in our own search for spiritual growth; and of course respect for the interdependent web of which we are all a part, a notion with its roots in virtually every world religion short of Christianity. Our call, our charge, is to figure out how to live our lives within this ethic of freedom and compassion and justice. How do we live a life that calls us to do what love requires?

One way is to make sure we have long memories. Today is August 6th, the 55th anniversary of the dropping of a horrible new weapon, curiously named "Little Boy", on Hiroshima. On the very last two pages of his book, in an appendix meant to contain case studies for further learning, Joseph Fletcher includes the following, as a case study in doing what love requires:

"Early on August 6, 1945, the Enola Gay lifted off the airstrip and a few hours later, in broad daylight, dropped a new weapon of mass extermination on unsuspecting Hiroshima. They had pretended to be on a routine weather mission. When the crew saw the explosion, they were silent. The Captain said simply, "my God, what have we done." Three days later another one fell on Nagasaki. About 152,000 men, women, and children were killed; many times more were wounded and burned, only to die later. The next day Japan surrendered."

Harry Truman had known nothing of the bomb until after his inauguration. A committee was appointed to decide how and when it would be used. Made up of distinguished and responsible people, they had a difficult time trying to agree on the terms of its use. Finally, in June of 1945, they reported to President Truman, recommending that a) the bomb be used against Japan as soon as possible, b) that it should be used against a dual target of military installations and civilian concentration, c) that it should be used without prior warning of its coming or its nature.

Finally, the President was faced with the final decision. At the White House with him were the Secretary of War, who vigorously defended the report as a whole; the Assistant Secretary, who was opposed; General Marshall, who was for it; Rear Admiral Strauss, who was against it; Scientist Enrico Fermi who was for it, and Scientist Leo Szilard who was against it. This was the moment of truth. Joseph Fletcher asks, "What does love require?"

Obviously, we know what decision was made, but was it the right one? I am sure that haunted President Truman all the days of his life that followed, regardless of the stoic face he painted for the electorate and for the historians. Making decisions about the living or dying of others is as hard as it gets, but guided by a liberal religious ethic of doing what love requires, of valuing the inherent worth and dignity of everything that lives, we can make easy and difficult decisions that resonate with our faith and that stand the test of time.

Late last Friday afternoon, when I had finally finished writing this sermon and hit the "save" key on my computer for the last time, I thought again of the recommendation I had made earlier in the day about withdrawing life support from the mentally retarded Hispanic woman with cerebral palsy. It was a moral and ethical recommendation and I did what love required. But then I thought that, perhaps, I had omitted one more thing that love required. And so I took my hospital stole, and my holy oil that a friend brought me back from Israel, and I went back to her room and said the prayers for anointing and healing of her Catholic faith, and made a sign of the cross on her forehead with that oil, and prayed for her to heal in mind, body, and spirit. I don't know if she could understand my English, or even if she knew I was there. I want so much to believe, whatever happens to her after she dies, that some freedom of the tortures of her mind and body will finally be hers. Her name is Criselda, and I hope that you will pray for her, too. Amen.

10

Weddings and Holy Unions

At the gathering, instrumental music is played which stops before the beginning, then continues with the bride or couple's entrance. After standing for the procession, all sit.

Welcome

Music or other personalized expression may be used here.

We have come together to witness the promises of
N. and N. in Marriage/Holy Union; to share with them in
their happiness and in their hopes for the future.

This partnership involves caring and giving. It involves
learning to share one's life with another person, forgiving
as the Universe forgives; enjoying the love and meaning
which can be found together. It involves facing together
whatever adversity may arise

Here before their friends and family, N. and N. wish to
pledge their love for each other and their desire to spend
their lives together.

Let us pray.

God of Love, we thank you
for the gift of companionship
and for the joy it brings.
We are grateful that you have brought us to this beautiful
moment, allowing us to share in your gifts of love and
relationship. Bless us as we share in this Union.
We thank you for the love
which has brought N. and N. to each other

and for their desire to share that love
for the rest of their lives. **Amen.**

Readings

*Appropriate readings, chosen or written by the
couple and read by persons also chosen by
them, may be included here.*

Interlude

*Music or other performance piece may be
included here.*

The Declarations

N. will you take N to be your friend and partner? Will
you share his joys and ease her burdens? Will you be
honest with him, and be faithful to her always, as long as
you both live?

Each partner answers: **I will.**

To the Families:

Are you willing to strengthen this Marriage/Union by
upholding both N. and N. with your love and concern?

We are.

To the whole group:

Will you, their friends and family, do all in your power to
support this couple now, and in the years ahead?
We will.

*If rings are used, they are brought forward here
and blessed. The couple then faces each other,
and each repeats the following:*

**N, today I take you to be my mate and partner.
Whatever life may bring,
I will love and care for you always.**

(place the ring on his/her finger)

**N., I give you this ring as a symbol of my vow,
and with all that I am, and all that I have, I honor
you, today and forever.**

We have witnessed the promises made by N. and N., and
now recognize them as joined in God's love.

If desired, all stand and lay hands on the couple.

Let us pray.

N. and N.,
you have committed yourselves
to one another in love,
joy, and tenderness.
Become one.
Fulfill your promises,
and may God's grace
be with you forever.
Amen.

Ladies and gentlemen, for their families (and for the State
of _____), I am honored to present to you
N. and N., now joined in marriage/holy union
The couple may kiss, and applause is customary.

11

Progressive Spirituality

While it may not have registered in the minds of most Unitarian Universalists, this past Wednesday was Ash Wednesday, the beginning of Lent in the Christian annual calendar. I am always amazed at how busy Ash Wednesday is for us at Grossmont Hospital. Of all the religious holidays, this is the one that I get the most calls about as chaplain there. Patients expect to have the ashes delivered to their rooms, and families and staff pack our extra-small chapel for the noontime service. This year we managed to impart ashes to at least 200 people, and we aren't even a church. I asked around, amazed as always, to see what it was that made this simple observance so popular. No one seemed to have the definitive answer, but all shared similar experiences. Our Catholic Priest even said that it's the busiest observance for most RC churches, taking on a cult or voodoo like importance to many Catholics, pious or not.

Ash Wednesday marks the beginning of the season of Lent, a traditional season of soul-searching and repentance, of reflection and taking stock, in the liturgical Christian tradition. Skipping Sundays, it is a forty-day period originating from the very earliest days of Christianity as a preparatory time for Easter, when the faithful rededicated themselves and when converts to the faith were prepared for Baptism, which would take place during the Great Vigil of Easter, or the Saturday night service before Easter Sunday. In many countries, the last day before Lent, called Mardi gras, Shrove Tuesday, or Carnival, has become a last fling before the solemn tone and fasting of the Lenten season. For centuries, it has been customary to fast by abstaining from meat during Lent, which is why some people call the festival Carnival, which is Latin for *farewell to meat*.

As I said before, the season itself lasts forty days, which is meant to be an imitation of the forty days that Jesus spent in the wilderness, according to the Gospel of Matthew, praying and fasting and being tempted by the devil. But forty days is also a traditional number of discipline, devotion, and preparation throughout Hebrew and Christian scripture. Moses stayed on the mountain forty days, Elijah traveled forty days before he reached the cave where he had his vision, and in the Book of Jonah, Nineveh was given forty days to repent. Still, the purpose of the Christian liturgical calendar is, of course, to relive the major events in Jesus' life in real time, which is the main reason that Lent lasts forty days.

Originally, the word "Lent" meant simply the spring season. I got to thinking about seasons, and how disconnected we have become at their nuances and changes. It seems at times that we live in such a fake world that we don't even need them. It's even more difficult here in San Diego, as our seasons change sometimes without any notice at all. Rising and setting, waxing and waning, labor and rest, sowing and reaping, light and dark, cold and hot. Birth, growth, decay, death. These things, in times gone by, once governed us. In my own theology, the Universe calls out to us in her splendor to not allow these things to pass us by without noticing them. It may be that in our noticing is where we might find some common ground, some common UU views of Lent.

Taken from Jesus' time of reflection in the desert, the Lenten season has evolved into a time of spiritual reflection and discernment for most Christian denominations and for many more people who simply want to set aside some special time to recognize their need for a good cleansing in the waters of their own inner spirituality. But how can such a time be useful to all of the continuums of belief that make up our Unitarian Universalist movement? Can an atheist or agnostic or humanist benefit from an exploration of spiritual disciplines in the same way that a Christian or Jew or Muslim or Hindu or Buddhist can?

In the past several weeks, the wonderful librarian at Grossmont Hospital has been gathering some articles for me as I prepare to write some grants to initiate several new projects in our chaplaincy program. One of those areas is in spiritual care education for nurses, as the nursing profession itself has recognized the need for effecting change in nurses' knowledge and understanding of the spiritual care requirements of patients. The librarian came upon a great article, by a nurse, which introduces a wonderful model for conducting this training. It begins with several definitions of spirituality, and it is in these definitions that I think a wide variety of Unitarian Universalists can find common ground.

The various definitions, found in the nursing literature that this article reviewed, are these:

1. Spirituality is the essence or life principle of a person.

2. Spirituality is a sacred journey.

3. Spirituality is the experience of the radical truth of things.

4.   Spirituality is how we go about giving meaning and purpose to life.

5.   Spirituality is a life relationship or a sense of connection with mystery, a higher power, God, or Universe.

6.   Spirituality is a belief or beliefs that relate a person to the world.

Finally, taking all these definitions and adding her own, the author of this article defined spirituality as rooted in an awareness which is part of the biological make up of the human species. Spirituality is therefore present in all individuals, and it may manifest as inner peace and strength derived from a perceived relationship with something that transcends the individual, such as a God or Ultimate Reality, the transcendent "other", as some people call it, or simply whatever an individual values as supreme. The spiritual dimension evokes feelings, which demonstrate the existence of love, faith, hope, trust, awe, and inspiration. This provides meaning and a reason for existence, and for many people our nurse author points out, it comes into focus when an individual faces stress, physical illness, or death.

The question that I want to take a little time to ask and answer is, if it is possible that there is room for some kind of spirituality across all of the beliefs in our UU movement, and given these definitions I believe that there **is** room, then what are some of the ways that we can embrace these 40 days and renew ourselves? How can we as Unitarian Universalists intensify our commitments, focus our activism, or sharpen our goal of building a community of diversity?

The Gospel of Matthew answers this question with the response in chapter 6, verses 1 through 18: summarized as *"give alms, pray to your creator, and fast without a gloomy face"*. I like the simplicity of give, pray, and fast, but I think they need some fine-tuning to be of any use to our diverse membership.

Almost every world religious teacher and leader, including Jesus, has taught that giving alms means making the needs of others our own, especially the needy of our community and our world. They are, of course, all around us every day. Children and the old, the sick and the suffering, families and individuals, next-door neighbors and people in lands far away, even walking in our own door and moving among us. In our busy days and busy lives we can forget them, but rather than looking out just for ourselves, try and see those in need, as Jesus says. Giving will make you live.

And how shall we give? Some time, some of our own talent, perhaps. Maybe some of our material resources, supporting national UU initiatives like the UUSC or local programs like Crisis House. Almsgiving is never just for the rich.

Poor or rich, we all have something to give. Whatever we give, though, should really be something of ourselves, something that costs us. We all know the paradoxical experience of how much more we seem to receive whenever we open up our hearts enough to give.

The Lenten season, in good Christian tradition, calls us to pray. According to Jesus, we should each "go into your room, and close the door, and pray to your Father in secret". Somehow I don't see too many of us doing this, but what is prayer if it isn't simply finding a way to connect with something beyond ourselves?

Two of my favorite movies of all time are "The Mission", with Jeremy Irons and Robert DiNiro, and "Gandhi", which won many Academy Awards including best picture, beating out "ET" as I recall, and best actor for Ben Kingsley. "The Mission" is a great story of archetypal conflict between colonists and natives, and also between a religious superior and a convert soldier turned Jesuit. A great line comes when Jeremy Irons, as the religious superior, opts for non-violence and says, "If the world has no place for love, then I don't want to live in it". "Gandhi", of course, is about the life of a prophet, a gospel on celluloid, who through the practice of nonviolence effects great political change.

The people depicted in these films share a burning desire for a vision of life that opened their minds and their hearts to live for others. They are certainly not alone. We hold up men and women throughout the ages as saints and models whose common thread is vision. In our UU movement we try very hard to explain away our extraordinarily small numbers by reminding ourselves of the great accomplishments of vision that famous Unitarian Universalists have contributed to our heritage. All these people had a vision that drove them to give the finest efforts of their lives so that others might live fully.

So maybe Lent is the most fitting time for us to connect with something larger than ourselves by asking the question, "What is my life's vision?" and taking that question into our hearts by being quiet with it in prayer, or in meditation, or alone on your favorite hike, or over coffee with your closest friend. Is there something that you believe in so strongly that you will dedicate everything you have to see it come to pass?

Lent is the time of the Vision Quest. It certainly was for the historical Jesus. He returned from his vision quest in the desert to Galilee, and according to Matthew, healed and cured the sick and preached perhaps his most famous sermon, calling upon his listeners to bless the poor and the meek and the merciful and the pure in heart and the peacemakers and those who mourn and those who hunger and thirst for righteousness, in other words, invite and include everyone to the table, even those who live on the margins of society. Quite a vision for only forty days.

Perhaps the most famous tradition associated with Lent, even to this day, is fasting. Scripture says, "When you fast do not look gloomy," but our society certainly looks on it as gloomy. Still, many people think about what they might give up for Lent, or fast from meat on Fridays. Self-denial is unfashionable in a time when we are urged to eat, drink, and buy more and more. Consumption is a habit taught us practically from childbirth, but most world religions teach that material possessions can turn into our captors. And as the resources of our planet are increasingly threatened, it becomes clear that the human family, especially those living in affluent nations, can no longer be unlimited consumers. We must develop a leaner, less wasteful way of life, if our planet is to survive.

So, what can we do to fast for our Lenten practice? Maybe use less water, installing dams in out toilets or watering the lawn less. Maybe remembering to turn off all the lights and save some energy, and give the money we save to Crisis House or our favorite charity. Maybe recycling. Maybe fasting from using our credit cards for 40 days, though I hate the thought of giving up any Southwest Airlines frequent flyer points by not using their card. Maybe by adopting a new habit that is healthy for our planet, and giving up an old one that isn't.

In this past Friday's edition of the San Diego Union Tribune, there was a cartoon that depicted a couple at home reading the paper in their living room. The husband turns to his wife and says, "What are you giving up for Lent?" and the wife, who is reading headlines that shout, "another shooting" or "more gun deaths" replies, "I am giving up hope". There is so much to be done in our broken society, including convincing people that it really is broken, that sometimes we can feel overwhelmed and hopeless. I know that many members and friends of the gay and lesbian community are feeling helpless and hopeless following the passage of Proposition 22 last Tuesday with such a convincing majority. But one of the things that embracing our own spirituality can do for us is help us to understand that we are never alone in our struggles for justice, another important and historical theme of the Lenten season, and that we will get up and brush ourselves off and live to work for change another day.

As Unitarian Universalists, we can take the traditional themes of Lent, giving, praying, and fasting, and turn them into Service and Vision and Stewardship. Deep down inside our marrow is the suspicion that everything matters. Our very instincts tell us that we can praise the Universe with everything that we do, that all of life is a great ceremony. Lent is the time when we recognize the beauty of sackcloth and ashes, when our metaphorical food is a plain contrast to the rich meats of feast times, when perhaps we can spend a little more time building our vision of how we want to be in the world.

Another of the customary scripture readings for Ash Wednesday is a short part of Paul's second letter to the Corinthians. Building upon the Lenten theme of self-sacrifice in the name of a just cause, I can hear in Paul's voice the voices of my own gay and lesbian brothers and sisters, and the voices of all the just across time who might embrace a common theme of service, vision and stewardship.

"As servants of God, we have commended ourselves in every way: through great endurance, in afflictions, hardships, calamities, beatings, imprisonments, riots, labors, sleepless nights, hunger; by purity, knowledge, patience, kindness, holiness of spirit, genuine love, truthful speech, and the power of God; with the weapons of righteousness for the right hand and for the left; in honor and dishonor, in ill repute and good repute. We are treated as imposters, and yet are true; as unknown, and yet are well known; as dying, and see we are alive; as punished, and yet not killed; as sorrowful, yet always rejoicing; as poor, yet making many rich; as having nothing, and yet possessing everything".

In this Lenten season, may whatever it is that you connect with beyond yourself give you grace to grow in service, insight to sharpen your vision, and generosity to expand your stewardship. As T.S. Eliot said, "we shall not cease from exploration, and the end of all our exploring shall be to arrive where we started, and know the place for the first time".

12

Celebrations of Life

◆

(Memorial Rituals)

Opening Poem and Welcome

This or other reading may be used

> Nature's first green is gold;
> Her hardest hue to hold.
> Her early leaf is a flower,
> but only so an hour.
>
> Then leaf subsides to leaf,
> So Eden sank to grief,
> So dawn goes down to day.
> Nothing Gold can stay.

* Musical Beginnings

Favorite music of the deceased is appropriate

* Invitation to the Spirit *(light main candle, if used)*

> Like the first disciples before the coming of God's love at
> Pentecost, we wait in faith, and pray.
> Be with us, Holy Spirit; nothing can separate us from
> your love. Be with us as of old, fill us with your power,
> direct all our thoughts to your goodness. Be present,
> Great Spirit; bring faith and healing and peace.

together to remember before God the life
nend him/her to God's keeping, and to
who mourn with our sympathy and with
: hope we share through the life and
example of jesus the Liberator.

God our Mother and Father,
we thank you that you have made each of us in your own
image, and given us gifts and talents with which to serve
creation. We thank you for N., the years we shared with
him/her, the good we saw in her/him, the love we
received from him/her. Now, give us the strength and
courage to leave him/her in your care, confident in your
promise of a wonderful life yet to come. **Amen.**

The Readings

*Up to three readings may be chosen, with very
brief commentary, preferably by different
persons known to the deceased, explaining the readings*

Musical Interlude

Homily/Eulogy

Sharing and Candle lighting

*This should be the main focus of the ritual and done
with great care. Everyone present is invited to share a story
or memory, or whatever may be on their heart. When
finished, they may light a candle as a symbol of
saying goodbye.*

Prayers of Goodbye

Let us pray.
N., we commit you to the keeping of Mother Earth, which
bears us all. We are glad that you lived, that we
saw your face, knew your friendship, and walked the way
of life with you. We deeply cherish the memory of your
words and deeds and character. We leave you in peace.

With respect we bid you farewell. In love we remember your companionship, your kindly ways. And thinking of you in this manner, we will go on in quietness of spirit and life in friendship with one another.

* Musical Ending

* Prayer of Letting Go and Blessing

Receive a blessing for all that may be required of you, that love may drive out fear, that you may be more perfectly abandoned to the will of God, and that peace and contentment may reign in your hearts, and through you may spread over the face of the earth.

The blessing of God: Giver of Life, Bearer of pain, Maker of Love, Creator and Sustainer, Liberator and Redeemer, Healer and Sanctifier, be with you all, and all whom you love, both living and departed, now and forever. Amen.

13

Why Christianity Must Change or Die

First, a reading from the letter of Paul to Titus.

From Paul, God's servant & an apostle of Jesus Christ, sent to strengthen the faith of those whom God has chosen and to promote their knowledge of the truth, which Godliness embodies, all in the hope of that eternal life which God promised before the ages began, and God can not lie. This is the appointed time, manifested in the teaching, manifested in the preaching entrusted to me by the command of God, our Savior.

To Titus, my own true child in our common faith, may grace and peace be yours from Abba God and Christ Jesus, our Savior.

The reason I left you in Crete was so that you might accomplish what had been left undone, especially the appointment of presbyters in every town. As I instructed you, presbyters must be irreproachable, married only once, and the parents of children who are believers and known not to be wild and insubordinate.

Now, bishops, as God's stewards, must be blameless. They must not be self willed or arrogant, addicted to drink, violent or greedy. On the contrary, they should be hospitable and love goodness and be steady, just, holy, and self-controlled. In their teachings they must hold fast the authentic message, so that they'll be able both to encourage the faithful to show sound doctrine and to refute those who contradict it.

This is necessary; frankly, because there are many rebellious types out there, idle talkers and deceivers, especially those who demand conversion to Judaism before becoming a Christian. They must be silenced for they are upsetting entire households by teaching things they shouldn't teach and doing it for financial gain. One of their own prophets once said, "Cretans have always been liars, evil animals, and lazy gluttons." This is a true statement. Therefore rebuke them sharply so that they'll be sound in the faith that should keep them from listening to empty myths and from heeding the commands of those who are no longer interested in the truth.

To the pure, all things are pure; but to those who are corrupted and lack faith, nothing can be pure. The corruption is both in their minds and in their consciences. They claim to know God while denying it with their actions. They are vile, disobedient, and quite incapable of doing good.

As for yourself, let your speech be consistent with sound doctrine. Tell your older people that they must be temperate, reserved, and moderate. They should be sound in faith, loving and steadfast. They must behave in ways that befit those who belong to God. They must not be slanderers or drunkards. By their good example, they must teach younger couples to love each other and their children, to be sensible, live pure lives, work hard, and be kind and submissive in their love relationships. In this way, the message of God will not fall into disgrace.

Tell young people to keep themselves completely under control, and be sure that you yourself set them a good example. Your teaching must have the integrity of serious, sound words to which no one can take exception. That way no opponent will be able to find anything bad to say about us, and hostility will yield to shame.

Tell workers that they're to obey their superiors and always do what they're told without arguing. And there must be no petty thieving. They must show complete honesty at all times. In this way they'll be a credit to the teaching of God, our Savior. The grace of God has appeared, offering salvation to all. It trains us to reject worldly desires and to live temperately, justly, and devoutly in this age as we await our blessed hope the appearing of the glory of our great God and our Savior Jesus Christ.

It was Christ who was sacrificed for us to redeem us from all unrighteousness and to cleanse the people to be Christ's own, eager to do what is right. Teach these things whether you are giving instructions or correcting errors. Act with full authority, and let no one despise you.

Now, to those of you who are guests this morning, no you have not stumbled into a Pentecostal Christian Church. Every year Summit Unitarian Universalist Fellowship holds a service auction, and in that service auction many different things are bid for articles of value and gifts of service a bartering, so to speak. One of the things that our senior minister, Ned Wight, and I always put up for sale is a customized sermon, and this morning I am delivering that customized sermon which was purchased by Dolores Moore.

Now, one of the things I'm very careful to do, whenever I do this service auction, is I never want to know how much the person paid for the sermon; because, frankly, it just puts way too much pressure on me. But Dolores, it turns out, is fascinated by Saint Paul.

Fascinated certainly doesn't mean that she agrees with him. In sending me the information that she wanted to give me about this sermon something of a three or four or five page e-mail, she said a couple of times, "Maybe I should stop now, because it sounds like I'm delivering your sermon for you. She says she's not particularly fond of Saint Paul, particularly because his attitude toward women raises all of her feminist hackles and I would have to agree with her. But she does ask some very interesting questions, specifically three that I want to address this morning.

1.   Did Paul ever say anything at all in his many writings that gives some clue to his sudden dramatic conversion?

2.   How many of Paul's teachings do you attribute to his honest personal belief system and how much to his role as a church father?

3.   How many times do you suppose Paul pushed an idea that was less a personal conviction and more something he thought would be to the benefit of the church?

In the reading from Titus we hear a typical voice of Saint Paul. It's a voice that's very rigid and very institutional. Saint Paul is clearly a company man. And one of the things to think about when you think about Saint Paul is that it's very important to contrast the things that he said with the teachings of Jesus. They are miles apart. And the central thesis of the sermon that I've worked out for Dolores today is that the work of Saint Paul must largely be discarded if the church, that is to say the Christian Church, is to survive another millennium.

The way that I'd like to do that this morning is to take a brief look at a little of the more recent history surrounding Saint Paul, some of the research that has been done. I think it might shed some light for us on where he was coming from, some of the things he meant. And then I want to look at how a changed Christianity might appear. And I'll do that using two visions. One is a vision of an Episcopal bishop, John Spong, and another is the vision of the large organization of biblical scholars called "the Jesus Seminar."

Recent research, recent books on the subject of Saint Paul have given us some modern insights to what might really have been going on in his life and in his ministry, and I want to share a few of those with you. It turns out that as a Christian missionary and theologian, Paul knew little and cared less about the life and teachings of Jesus of Nazareth. Much more important in Paul's mind was the death and resurrection of the exalted Christ who appeared to him in a mystical vision. He was intensely apocalyptic and believed that Christ's second coming was immanent. Consequently, he did not intend his sometimes stern judgments on doctrinal matters and on issues of gender and sexuality to become church dogma, applied, as they have been, with horrible and bloody results, for the last two thousand years. Although an apostle to the Gentiles, Paul remained thoroughly Jewish in his outlook and saw the Christian movement as a means of expanding and reforming traditional Judaism. He had no thought of starting a new religion.

For all his energy and influence, Paul wrote only a fraction of the New Testament letters that tradition ascribes to him. He probably did not write the letter that I read this morning and even some of those were altered by others to reflect later developments in church theology. So, Paul gets a little of the blame, but not all of the blame.

Most of what we know about Paul comes from his own writings and from the Acts of the Apostles, a New Testament chronicle, of course, of the early church, written many decades after Paul's death. Though none of the writings are truly biographical, they provide revealing glimpses into his life and career.

The story is fairly familiar to most people. He was born Saul in the town of Tarsus, in what is now southern Turkey, probably in about AD 10. He joined a sect of Pharisees, something we could describe as strict constructionists of the Judaic laws. Writing years later to Christians in Phillipi, Paul probably recounted his ethnic credentials. "Circumcised on the eighth day; a member of the people of Israel of the tribe of Benjamin; a Hebrew born of Hebrews; as to the law, a Pharisee, as to zeal, a persecutor of the church; as to righteousness under the law, absolutely blameless."

In spite of the things that are written, we don't know very much about his physical traits. In one of his letters to the Corinthians, he speaks vaguely of a physical affliction, a "thorn in the flesh," that he describes as "a messenger of Satan to torment me, to keep me from being too elated." Biblical scholars have speculated many things about this. It could have been a physical issue, such as epilepsy, malaria, or some sort of an eye disease, while Bishop John Spong in his book, Rescuing the Bible from Fundamentalism, suggests that Paul was a repressed and self-loathing homosexual, and that's what he was describing in his letter to the Corinthians.

In his early career, according to both Acts and his own letters, he was a zealous persecutor of Christians. Some scholars now believe he was a member of a radical and sometimes violent faction of a small group of Pharisees. His career as a persecutor of Christians came to a dramatic end in the story that Dolores alluded to in her e-mail to me. On the road to Damascus, as the book of Acts tells it, he had a vision: "A light from heaven flashed around him. He fell to the ground and heard a voice saying to him, 'Saul, Saul, why do you persecute me?' He asked, 'Who are you, Lord?' The reply came, 'I am Jesus, whom you are persecuting, but get up and enter the city, and you will be told what you are to do.'"

He is temporarily blinded. He is led away by his traveling companions to Damascus. According to the text, there he's filled with the Holy Spirit. He regains his sight, he is baptized, and immediately begins proclaiming Jesus as the Son of God. He has received his call to be a witness to all the world and an apostle to the Gentiles. He, at this point, really believed that God had indeed begun to inaugurate a new age for Israel, just as the followers of Jesus whom he had persecuted had so passionately proclaimed.

Through his own direct encounter, his own described direct encounter with the risen Christ, say many scholars, he became convinced that Jesus earlier incarnation as a poor Galilean peasant was merely a prelude to his revelation as Israel's Messianic redeemer, which of course is spoken of in Hebrew scriptures.

He began many campaigns to convert. He did so without ever having known Jesus, without largely knowing, perhaps, what many of Jesus' teachings were. He walked down a completely separate path. That's a very important concept for us to get. It's a very important concept to understand the journey that the Christian church has taken since Paul's time.

So, what he actually did was separate from the movement that Jesus had begun. He would be called into Rome at one point to address who he was before Peter, and they came to some conclusions; but, of course, the whole church changed shortly after that became the official religion of Rome, and the Christian church as we now know it was well on its way to how we see it today.

I'm struck whenever I review this, as I know Dolores was struck, by how different these visions were: Jesus' vision versus Paul's vision, and the many church followers that came after Paul. And much has happened in those two thousand years since, but as we find ourselves now in 1999, we find ourselves with many movements in the Christian church who are claiming that the church must change or die. It must radically alter what it is, what it means to people, and I want to suggest that one of the most important movements that can help make that happen is the Unitarian Universalist movement. We are one of the few organized religions that can address these issues with integrity. Other churches certainly try, and I want to share two of those other visions of what a changed Christianity might look like.

The first is of an Episcopal bishop, John Shelby Spong, when he asked the question, "Can one be a Christian without being a theist?" And he describes theism this way, "Theism is the historic way men and women have been taught to think about God. Most people think theism is the only conceivable way to think about God. The primary image of God in the Bible is a theistic image." For him "a theistic God is a God conceived of as a being, even a Supreme Being, external to this world, supernatural in power, and operating on this world in some fashion to call this world and those of us who inhabit it into the divine will or the divine presence. This theistic being is inevitably portrayed in human terms, as a person who has a will, who loves, who rewards and who punishes. One can find other images of God in the scriptures, but this is the predominant and the familiar one."

Spong goes on to argue that the possibility of being a Christian without being a theist can only be possible in a world that renders a traditional theistic view of God inoperative, and many of the ways that that definition evolves as inoperative are provided by the Jesus Seminar.

For those of you who aren't familiar with the Jesus Seminar, it's a group of mostly New Testament scholars who have been working together now for almost ten years. They come from many different faiths and traditions. The press likes to portray them as liberal, but it's not necessarily so. They have come together to do a number of tasks, the most important of which has been to try to determine what Jesus actually said and what Jesus actually did.

The founder of their movement, Robert Funk, has come up with some theses of what he calls "the coming radical reformation," not unlike the theses that Luther nailed to the Wittenberg door, Funk has twenty-one. They're brief, and I want to review them very quickly. They're very radical, and they're very interesting. I think they offer promise in terms of where Christianity can go in the new millennium.

1. The God of the metaphysical age is dead. There is not a personal God out there external to human beings in the material world. We must reckon with a deep crisis in God-talk and replace it with talk about whether the universe has meaning and whether human life has purpose.

2. The doctrine of special creation of the species died with the advent of Darwinism and the new understanding of the age of the earth and magnitude of the physical universe. Special creation goes together with the notion that the earth and human beings are at the center of the galaxy. The demise of a geocentric universe took the doctrine of special creation with it.

3. The deliteralization of the story of Adam and Eve in Genesis brought and end to the dogma of original sin as something inherited from the first human

being. Death is not punishment for sin but is entirely natural, and sin is not transmitted from generation to generation by means of male sperm as suggested by Augustine.

4. The notion that God interferes with the order of nature from time to time in order to aid or punish is no longer credible, in spite of the fact that most people still believe it.

5. Prayer is meaningless when understood as requests (suggests?) to an external God for favor or forgiveness and meaningless if God does not interfere with the laws of nature. Prayer as praise is a remnant of the age of kingship in the ancient near east and is beneath the dignity of deity. Prayer should be understood principally as meditation, as listening rather than talking, and as attention to the needs of neighbor.

6. We should give Jesus a demotion. It is no longer credible to think of Jesus as divine. Jesus' divinity goes together with the old theistic way of thinking about God.

7. The plot early Christians invented for a divine redeemer figure is as archaic as the mythology in which it is framed. A Jesus who drops down out of heaven, performs some magical act that frees human beings from the power of sin, rises from the dead, and returns to heaven, is simply no longer credible. The notion that he will return at the end of time and sit in cosmic judgment is equally incredible. We must find a new plot for a more credible Jesus.

8. The virgin birth of Jesus is an insult to modern intelligence and should be abandoned. In addition, it is a pernicious doctrine that denigrates women.

The theses go on to talk about areas of God's domain according to Jesus. They talk about the canon, and one of my favorite areas, Number 19, the New Testament, as a highly uneven and biased record of orthodox attempts to invent Christianity. The canon of scripture adopted by traditional Christianity should be contracted and expanded simultaneously to reflect respect for the old tradition and open us to the new.

Only the works of strong poets, those who startle us, amaze us with a glimpse of what lies beyond the range of present sight should be considered for inclusion. The canon should be a collection of scriptures without a fixed text and without either insider or outside limits, like the myth of King Arthur and the Knights of the Round Table or the myth of the American west.

And finally they talk about the language of faith. In re-articulating the vision of Jesus, we should take care to express ourselves in the same register as he employed in his parables and aphorisms, paradox, hyperbole, exaggeration, and metaphor. In other words, artistic expression poetry. Further, our reconstructions of his visions should be provisional, always subject to modification and correction.

So, Dolores asked us, "Did Paul ever say anything at all in his many writings that give some clue to his sudden dramatic conversion?" No. She asked us, "How many of Paul's teachings do you attribute to his honest personal belief system and how many to his role as church father?" I attribute all his teachings to his belief system. And three, she asks, "How many times do you suppose Paul pushed an idea that was less a personal conviction and more something he felt would be to the benefit of the church?" I think he always pushed his personal conviction.

But his conviction was a completely different path, I would argue, than Jesus would have taken; and it took us in the direction of a completely different church than Jesus would have started if, in fact, Jesus ever thought of starting a church. Let's not forget that Jesus was a Jew, and there's absolutely nothing in his teachings that indicates that a new church should be started in his name.

Having said all this, I want once again to make a plea that we as Unitarian Universalists won't continue to discard Christianity as useless to our spiritual journeys. I'm not ready to give up on Jesus, and I'm not ready to give up on Jesus' teachings. They are part of my heritage. In many ways, they are how I describe myself. I think they're important to our UU heritage, and we can't just discard them in other words, throwing the baby out with the bath water because we don't like Paul.

It seems to me that many Christians are so engrossed in the birth and death stories of Jesus that they forget what happened in between. While they find a sincere religious experience in their belief in the divine risen Christ, I can find, and I hope someday we all can find, an equally sincere belief in the human Jesus who gave himself totally to the divinity that is inside each and every one of us.

14

The Sacrament of Foot washing

Foot washing recalls the example of Jesus' humility as Good Friday drew near and Jesus performed this domestic chore for his protesting disciples, according to the Gospel of John (13:1-17). It was the custom in the ancient world that provision be made for the feet of guests to be bathed when they arrived at the home of their host. Servants or people of low rank in the larger family ordinarily did this task.

We observe foot washing because Jesus offered it as an example of radical humility and service, traditions that are central to our Thomas Christian heritage and belief. It is not itself the only or highest example of humility and service, but symbolically it demonstrates them in great power.

A service of foot washing may be held at any time, but it is traditionally included in the evening service of Maundy Thursday in holy week. It is also particularly appropriate to use in a service of commissioning or ordination, as the ordaining persons wash the feet of those they are about to ordain as a symbol of the radical egalitarian nature of Thomas Christians.

Opening Words

God is spirit, and those who worship God
should worship in spirit and in truth.

We come together with thanks and praise.

My brothers and sisters, our help is in the name of the
eternal God.

Who is making the heavens and the earth.

Telling the Story

It was now the day before the Passover festival.
Jesus and his disciples were at supper. Jesus rose
from the table, took off his outer garment, and

tied a towel around his waist. Then Jesus poured
some water into a washbasin and began to wash the
disciples' feet and dry them with the towel around
his waist.

Are you going to wash my feet, Lord?

Jesus answered Peter:

**You do not understand now what I am doing,
but you will understand later.**

After washing their feet, Jesus put the outer
garment back on, returned to his place at the table,
and said "do you understand what I have just done
to you?"

**You call me Teacher and Lord, and it
is right that you do so, because that is
what I am. I, your Lord and Teacher, have
just washed your feet. You, then, should wash
one another's feet. I have set an example for
you, so that you will do for others what I
have done for you".**

*A period of silence should follow here before
the story is concluded.*

Jesus said: I am telling you the truth. No slave is
greater than the master who is served, and no
messenger is greater than the one who sends the
message. Now that you know this truth, how happy
you will be if you put it into practice.

**Now, as Jesus taught, we share the
water of humility, and stoop,
as Jesus once stooped,
to wash the feet of others.**

*In silence or with soft background music, the
foot washing takes place here.*

*When this service takes place alone, it may
be concluded here with a hymn and benediction, When
part of another service, refer to the appropriate page
number to continue.*

15

Trends in Progressive Christianity

This morning I'd like to share with you some of my reflections on the small but growing movement called progressive Christianity. No, I am not here to convert you, and in spite of our surroundings there will be no revivals or alter calls. There **will** be an ancient practice of hospitality called communion or Eucharist, actually just a Passover meal with a twist, but I'll talk about that later. In the meantime, I invite you to join me in this conversation even if your own beliefs are far, far away from any kind of Christianity that you can imagine. I promise to hold the beliefs you feel in your heart with gentleness and respect even as I share the deepest beliefs of my own heart.

I suppose like any good community of Unitarian Universalists I could poll you all right now and I'd probably get at least 100 different definitions of Christianity as well as progressive Christianity. We are an opinionated bunch aren't we? But let me share with you the definition of this movement put forward by the Center for Progressive Christianity, likely the leading voice in the movement right now. They have defined it in terms of eight "points". By calling oneself "progressive we mean that we are Christians who: 1) acknowledge that we have found our own, personal understanding of Divinity through the life and teachings of Jesus; 2) that we respect people who follow other ways to God or other ways to their own spirituality and we acknowledge that their ways are as true for them as our way is true for us; 3) that we understand that those of us who share bread and wine in Jesus' name are holding up an ancient vision of all people being welcome at the same table, no matter who they are or where they come from; 4) that we invite people of all kinds to participate in our spiritual and social life without insisting that they become like us in order to be acceptable, and by all kinds we mean believers and agnostics, skeptics, women and men equally, those who are gay, lesbian, bisexual, and Tran gendered as well as those who are straight, those who hope for a better world and those who have lost hope, and those of all races and cultures and all classes and abilities; 5) That the way we behave toward one another and toward other people is way more important than the way we talk about our beliefs; 6) that we find more promise in the quest for understanding than we do in absolute certainty, and more value in the questions than in the answers; 7) that in community together we try to equip one another for the work we feel called to do, trying to assure justice and peace for all people and bringing hope to those who have lost hope; 8) that we recognize that this path can be costly because we are called to resist all unethical actions in the private sector and in government, a tradition that has been honored whenever the collective church has been its most faithful.

The thing I like best about this rather long definition is that nowhere in it will you find the centuries of layered theology that the institutional Christian church has conjured up to maintain its prestige and power for over 2000 years. Nowhere in it will you find the kind of patriarchal arrogance we see even today in the Roman church. Nowhere in it do we claim the bible as infallible and all non-believers heretics. Nowhere in it do we strip anyone of their humanity, as the church has always done to those it wants to dehumanize or exclude. What we do find within it are the basic teachings of a wandering Jew named Jesus, and it should come as no surprise to any of us that those teachings bear a striking resemblance to our own Unitarian Universalist Principles and Purposes.

The other thing we find within that definition is the heart of Jesus the Healer, and I want to draw that out a bit more with you this morning because it seems as though the humanity of Jesus is at the heart of the progressive movement today and the heart of Jesus' teachings really is his work as a healer and reconciler.

According to Christian scripture, Jesus heals many bodily ailments, including fever, paralysis, leprosy, blindness, deafness, a withered hand, excessive menstrual bleeding, edema, and other illnesses. Of course, it is not always possible to equate first or second-century descriptions with modern classifications of diseases. These healings of the body took place through words and touch. The rituals were simple, the words had no real magical quality to them, and occasionally an anointing took place, often with saliva and perhaps some dirt. The question we must ask ourselves is, how should we understand, from the words given us in ancient texts, the way in which Jesus' healing took place?

Some scholars say that if Jesus healed ailments such as the ones I've mentioned, then those cases were of a certain sort, not just any disorders but disorders of the kind that can be healed, on the spot, by the words or the self-presentation of the healer. They regard these disorders as psychosomatic in nature or, more precisely, as conversion disorders in which a person converts a psychological problem into a physical manifestation, something we call somatic disorders. As progressive scholars see it, Jesus heals through the modality of forgiveness. One classic example of healing through forgiveness is the story of the paralytic whose pallet is lowered through the roof into Jesus' presence, as told in the Gospel of Mark:

"A few days later, when Jesus again entered Capernaum, the people heard that he had come home. So many gathered that there was no room left, not even outside the door, and he preached the word to them. Some men came, bringing to him a paralytic, carried by four of them. Since they could not get him to Jesus because of the crowd, they made an opening in the roof above Jesus and, after digging through it, lowered the mat the paralyzed man was lying on. When Jesus saw their faith, he said to the paralytic, "Son, your sins are forgiven." Now some teachers of the law were sitting there, thinking to themselves, "Why does this fellow talk like that? He's blaspheming! Who can forgive sins but God alone?" Immediately Jesus knew in his spirit that this was what they were thinking in their hearts, and he said to them, "Why are you thinking these things? Which is easier: to say to the paralytic, 'Your sins are forgiven,' or to say, 'Get up, take your mat and walk'? But that you may know that the Son of Man has authority on earth to forgive sins…." He said to the paralytic, "I tell you, get up, take your mat and go home." He got up, took his mat and walked out in full view of them all. This amazed everyone and they praised God, saying, "We have never seen anything like this!"

What are we to make of this explanation of Jesus' healings? On the one hand, the fact that this is the only story in Christian scripture linking forgiveness with healing of disease makes it a slim basis upon which to generalize about Jesus as a healer. On the other hand, conversion and somatic disorders must have occurred then as now. Just as Jesus addressed the issue of forgiveness with this man, which may have been the key to his cure, there is a role to be played today by a spiritual ministry that addresses guilt and forgiveness. Certainly the Roman Catholics think so in their sacraments of confession and absolution, and it is also a central feature of many 12-step programs such as Alcoholics Anonymous. Think about your own life for a moment. Have you ever felt healed by the act of releasing guilt or shame, or even by releasing it within yourself, or by asking another for their forgiveness? If healing is the central theme of Jesus' ministry, then unconditional forgiveness comes in a close second. As a chaplain, I have to ask myself if this doesn't suggest a wider role for clergy, pastoral counselors, and chaplains in the healing of physical illness.

I also have to ask myself about the power of prayer to heal, and it seems to me that this needs to be explained in two different ways. First, if the person who is experiencing the healing can hear my prayer, and my references to forgiveness, and therefore feels that forgiveness as a result of that prayer, then what I have just said about forgiveness makes sense. But how do we explain randomized, controlled, double-blind, prospective, parallel-group studies like the one published a little over a year ago in the Archives of Internal Medicine, which demonstrated that intercessory prayer, or praying for others who were ill without their knowledge, was clearly associated with a better medical outcome in cardiac patients? More studies are obviously needed here, but this is about the third or fourth time this particular model has been replicated. At Grossmont Hospital, where I serve as chaplain, we will hopefully begin a similar 12-month study to see if there is any connection between pain control and prayer in orthopedic post-operative patients. Stay tuned for the results.

There is another dimension, another perspective if you will, of Jesus' healing ministry that has not been written about much but which hospital chaplain Robert Richardson discusses in his recent article called "An Image of Holistic Care for the Sick," and that is the social implications of Jesus' healings. In the healing stories of the gospel, many portray the social situation of those who came for healing, demonstrating Jesus' attention to the poor and those who had no access to health care, to beggars, to widows, and to outcasts. These stories also differentiate Jesus from other healers who were his contemporaries, and many form the basis of how we think of ourselves today as progressive Christians.

The sick in Jesus' day were stigmatized and subject to social discrimination, conditions that we can relate to in our own time with the plagues of polio and AIDS. In his time and in ours, to put an end to this discrimination was an act of social criticism, which was an important part of Jesus' healing work. Social medicine has shown how unjust circumstances contribute to making people ill, so it is often impossible to heal the sick without healing their relationships, the circumstances in which they live, and the structures of the social system to which they belong.

The gospel of Mark is literally filled with stories of the social dimension of Jesus' healing. We have heard about the paralytic, unable to walk and dependent upon his litter bearers. There is the bricklayer with a withered hand, who would be handicapped from working. There is the possessed Gerasene man, a homeless person living among the tombs, a place of uncleanness and death. There is the woman with a hemorrhage, unclean as far as sexual relations are concerned and unclean religiously. And there is the leper, isolated from society and from religious participation, in chapter 1:

"A man with leprosy came to him and begged him on his knees, "If you are willing, you can make me clean." Filled with compassion, Jesus reached out his hand and touched the man. "I am willing," he said. "Be clean!" Immediately the leprosy left him and he was cured. Jesus sent him away at once with a strong warning: "See that you don't tell this to anyone. But go, show yourself to the priest and offer the sacrifices that Moses commanded for your cleansing, as a testimony to them." Instead he went out and began to talk freely, spreading the news. As a result, Jesus could no longer enter a town openly but stayed outside in lonely places. Yet the people still came to him from everywhere."

These are the people to whom Jesus went or who approached him. Few would have access to physicians, and few were persons of power and authority. Jesus did not refuse healing to the rich and powerful, so he healed both the woman who had spent all her money on physicians and the daughter of the chief rabbi of the synagogue. Jesus healed across social and religious boundaries, and did not hesitate to touch those who the social structure of his day perceived to be unclean, whether due to hemorrhage, leprosy, or spirit. He touches the untouchables, and they are healed. He offers forgiveness, and the demons flee. But as the sad end of his story shows, physical and mental illness flee before him more readily than the domination systems of society and institutional religion. The more things change, it seems, the more they stay the same.

Most kids in school know the story of Helen Keller, whose dark and silent world was finally penetrated by her teacher, Anne Sullivan. What many kids don't know about Keller is that she graduated from Radcliff, became a radical socialist, and addressed the social causes of blindness and the exploitation of workers and of women. To follow the image of Jesus as healer today means to go beyond the miracle worker to the hard work of social healing.

So far, I haven't said much about faith, or spiritual healing. I know what spiritual care is, and I think I know what spiritual healing is, too. For me, spiritual care is helping someone use their faith, whatever that faith may be, in the service of their own healing. Spiritual healing is when wholeness is restored. When he healed, Jesus often finished with the words "go now, your faith had made you whole." Like any good hospital chaplain, he doesn't specify what faith that might be or require adherence to a doctrine or dogma before he offers healing to others. It is an unconditional gift. Perhaps the most powerful gift we can give another is unconditional presence, unconditional acceptance, unconditional forgiveness, and unconditional love. Physical, mental, societal, and spiritual healing are available to us, and we can all affirm Jesus' example as a healer as a way to move toward those goals, regardless of our personal faith or belief.

The Jesus of progressive Christianity is fully a man, fully human, a teacher, prophet and healer. His divinity is a reflection of our own, a reflection of holiness found throughout creation. When we share bread and juice in a few moments, it will not be because I have magically transformed those things into the body and blood of Jesus. It will not be because the only way to salvation is through Jesus and the institutional structures that have been built and maintained for thousands of years in his name. It will not be because you feel some obligation to do it to avoid being shunned by God, and it will not be because your parents are making you do it because its what everybody in your family has always done.

We will share bread and juice to imitate the simplest and most holy of acts; to announce to ourselves and to everyone around us that every time we remember Jesus in this special way we are affirming our Unitarian Universalist belief in the inherent worth and dignity of every person and their right to be included at the table of humanity. That simple act is called hospitality, and it is one of the central themes throughout Judeo-Christian scripture. It is one of the hallmarks of what it means to be a progressive Christian, the re-discovery of the simple themes of Jesus' teachings.

That journey of discovery is something we can all participate in regardless of our specific religious belief. Maybe those of us who have been hurt or damaged by the traditional church can reclaim the faith that is our birthright simply by studying the teachings of Jesus in the same way we study the divine teachings of other world religious leaders.

For some of us, that journey of discovery has defined who we are. I knew I was meant to be a hospital chaplain when I began working with AIDS patients in the late eighties. It was as clear as day, no discernment required. I get to help people make meaning out of the most meaningful events of their lives. I had a chance to see the Broadway version of The Lion King a few months ago, and the character I always identify with most is Rafiki, the medicine man or shaman. The actor who plays Rafiki is a woman, which I think is particularly appropriate. Rafiki is a storyteller, a keeper of the traditions, a healer who stays off to the side and out of the limelight but is always there when needed somehow and is never afraid to take a stand or lead the way when necessary.

To say that I became a minister because I want to help people seems too simple. I became a minister because I knew I had to and now I can't imagine being anything else. It is my progressive understanding of the teachings of Jesus that drives my ministry, and gives me hope for a healed world. May something of this new progressive movement, still in its infancy, speak to your heart and help illuminate your path. And as Nancy Wood says, may you hold on to what you believe, even if it is a tree which stands by itself. Amen.

16

Rituals of Naming and Baptism

Opening Words

The poet e.e. cummings reminds us: "we can never be born enough. We are human beings for whom birth is a supremely welcome mystery. The mystery of growing, the mystery which happens only and whenever we are faithful to ourselves. Life for eternal us is now."

Responsive Reading

This is a time for joy. We rejoice when a child is born into the care and concern, not only of parents, but also of our community.

In welcoming a child, we celebrate the miracle of birth.

Every child born into the world needs the love and care of others. Each deserves to be held in loving arms and to be taught good ways of living.

Each child has the right to know what it means to be human and what we must do to make life beautiful and good for ourselves, for each other, and for all the living beings who share this earth home with us.

In welcoming a child, we celebrate our hopes for life.

Address to Parents/Guardians

N. and N., in presenting your child today, you invite all of us to share some of the joy and responsibility that is yours as parents. You seek our support in your dedication to the task of fostering, with love and guidance, the fullest unfolding of the personality of your child.

Do you now promise that, to the best of your human abilities, you will help this child to an appreciation of truth and beauty, uprightness of character, and of love?

We do.

Address to Godparents

N. and N., an old Jewish proverb says, "In time of travail, go to the friend of your father, go to the friend of your mother." From this ancient wisdom comes the idea of godparents, or special people who dedicate themselves to watching out for the welfare of others' children. It is a noble and loving tradition to which you commit yourselves today.

Do you then, to the best of your abilities, intend to supplement the care and love of these parents, both in the day to day development of this child, and especially in the event of any extraordinary need?

We do.

Meditation

Let us pray.
Spirit of life, we are your children. Out of the infinite we have come to you and through you. We are the old, yet ever new miracle of incarnation. Give us a chance to grow, within the warmth of your unfailing love, into souls sensitive to beauty, hearts open to love and hungry for the religious and spiritual values of life. Do not shrink and wither us with fear, but quicken with faith the springs of courage within us. Enter with us through the gates of wonder, into the wider universe. Accept us as we grow into a community

of mutual respect and shared responsibility, that
we in our turn may be worthy parents of the
coming generation. Amen.

Naming and Dedication/Baptism

N. and N., by what name is this child known?

*Parents/guardians give complete name of child
Leader dips fingers in holy water and touches
child's forehead:*
I touch your young brow with water from old
nature's infinite sky, water that touches every
shore and nourishes every race of people. In so
doing I dedicate your life and thought to the good of
all humankind and to your own true growing (and I
baptize you in the name of the God the Creator,
Jesus the Redeemer, and Eternal Spirit). Amen.

Leader gives child or parents a flower:
I also give you this flower, unique in all its natural
beauty, separate and distinct from all other flowers
found in creation, to express symbolically our hope
that all your life long you will unfold and blossom
just as you must, in all of your own unique and
natural beauty.

*Leader may anoint forehead with oil, or simply
place hand on child's head as the following is said:*
May the blessings of an understanding heart, strength
and integrity of purpose, and love received and given,
be yours and remain with you as you go forward
into ever fuller life. Amen.

APPENDIX A

Calendar of Observances

January

1   The naming of Jesus
Emancipation Proclamation (1863)
New Year's Day, celebration of peace with
all creation.

3   Death of Joy Adamson in Kenya

3   Birthday of J.R.R. Tolkien (1892)

4   Albert Camus, man of goodwill (1960)

5   Twelfth Night, Eve of the Feast of the Magi

6   Epiphany

8   Galileo Galilei, observer of creation (1642)

12   George Fox, founder of the Quakers (1691)

14   Birthday of Albert Schweitzer, humanitarian

15   Birthday of Martin Luther King, Jr. (1929)

17   Yearly migration of Grey Whales

22   Surrender of lands by Chief Seattle (1854)

30   Gandhi, apostle of nonviolence (1948)

Full Moon Day: The Wolf Moon, time to remember
the hungry and homeless of the earth.

February

2	The Presentation of Jesus
2	Candlemas Day
4	Comet Halley appears (1531)
12	Festival of Diana, goddess protector Birthday of Abraham Lincoln
14	Valentine of Terni, bishop and martyr (270)
19	Michelangelo, artist of humanity (1564)
20	Frederick Douglass, black liberator (1895)
21	Murder of Malcolm X (1965)
23	Supernova 1987, Festival of the Exploding Stars

Full Moon Day: The Snow Moon

March

8	International Women's Day
14	Birthday of Albert Einstein
17	Patrick, bishop (461)
21	Spring Equinox Innocents of Sharpville, South Africa (1960)
25	Feast of the Annunciation Death of Ishi, last Native American (1916)
26	Walt Whitman, poet (1892)
30	Jesus the runaway

Full Moon Day: The Worm Moon, day of prayers
for preparation of soil.

April

7	World Health Day
8	Celebration of Buddha's Birthday
9	Dietrich Bonhoeffer, revolutionary (1945)
10	Pierre Teilhard de Chardin (1955)
15	Damien, priest, leper, and healer
22	International Earth Day

Full Moon Day: The Pink Moon, time when earth is in the pink of health and vitality

May

1	Beltane, or May Day Festival
1	Jesus the Worker: International Workers Day
2	Leonardo da Vinci, artist and inventor (1519)
5	Student martyrs of Kent, Ohio (1970)
18	Festival of Pan, Greek celebration of all that is male in the universe
19	Marcia Herndon, bishop and teacher (1997)
24	Nicolas Copernicus, astronomer (1543)
31	Visitation of Mary, bearer of Jesus

Full Moon Day: The Full Flower Moon or the Corn Planting Moon

June

1	First Negro Slaves arrive in Virginia (1619)
5	Robert F. Kennedy (1968)
6	Phillip the Deacon
7	Death of the Prophet Mohammed (632)

20   Midsummer's Eve

21   Summer Solstice

24   John the Baptizer

27   Innocents of Dachau, Auschwitz, other camps

27   Stonewall Riots, New York City (1969)

29   The Holy Apostles

Full Moon Day: Strawberry Moon or Rose Moon

July

3   Green Corn Dance, festival of first harvest

4   U.S. Independence Day

6   Isaiah, prophet

12   Birthday of Henry David Thoreau

16   Meister Eckhart, mystic (1328)

20   First Moon Landing (1969)

Full Moon Day: The Thunder Moon, prayer for rain
for this season's crops

August

1   Lammas, Festival of New Bread and Harvest

1   Mikhail Itkin, bishop and activist (1989)

6   Transfiguration of Jesus

6   Innocents of Hiroshima (1945)

9   Innocents of Nagasaki

15   Assumption of the Virgin Mary

16   Ulric Vernon Herford, bishop (1938)

20   Jonathan Daniels, martyr of Selma (1965)

Full Moon Day: The Red Moon

September

16   United Nations International Day of Peace

22   Autumnal Equinox

23   Worldwide Day of Prayer to heal Mother Earth

29   Michaelmas Day

Full Moon Day: The Harvest Moon

October

4   Feast of St. Francis of Assisi (1226)

5   Teresa of Avila, visionary (1582)

16   United Nations World Food Day

19   Nikos Kazantzakis, prophet (1957)

25   Birthday of Pablo Picasso (1881)

31   Samhain, All Hallow's Eve

Full Moon Day: The Hunter's Moon

November

1   Festival of All Saints

1   First Day of Dios de los Muetos (The Days of the Dead)

2   Festival of All Souls

2   Second Day of Dios de los Muertos

8   Birthday of Dorothy Day (1897)

9   Berlin Wall came down (1989)

11   Martinmas, final harvest festival

15   International Fast for a World Harvest (Oxfam)

22   John Fitzgerald Kennedy (1963)

27   Harvey Milk, George Moscone; martyrs
        for gay and lesbian rights (1978)

Full Moon day; The Beaver Moon, time of
preparation for winter and reminder to recreate
ourselves.

December

1   World AIDS Day

6   Nicholas of Myra, bishop (325)

10   International Human Rights Day

13   Feast of St. Lucia, northern Europe

16   Mexican Posadas Celebration begins

21   Winter Solstice, or Yule

21   Thomas, apostle
        Annual Festival and Remembrance Day for
        Thomas Christians worldwide.

24   Eve of the birth of Jesus

25   Birthday of Jesus, beginning 12 days of
        celebration of the coming of light

28   Holy Innocents throughout the World

Full Moon Day: The Cold Moon

APPENDIX B

The Gospel of Thomas

These are the secret sayings that the living Jesus spoke and Didymos Judas Thomas recorded.

1 And he said, "Whoever discovers the interpretation of these sayings will not taste death."

2 Jesus said, "Those who seek should not stop seeking until they find. When they find, they will be disturbed. When they are disturbed, they will marvel, and will reign over all. [And after they have reigned they will rest.]"

3 Jesus said, "If your leaders say to you, 'Look, the (Father's) kingdom is in the sky,' then the birds of the sky will precede you. If they say to you, 'It is in the sea,' then the fish will precede you. Rather, the kingdom is within you and it is outside you. When you know yourselves, then you will be known, and you will understand that you are children of the living Father. But if you do not know yourselves, then you live in poverty, and you are the poverty."

4 Jesus said, "The person old in days won't hesitate to ask a little child seven days old about the place of life, and that person will live. For many of the first will be last, and will become a single one."

5 Jesus said, "Know what is in front of your face, and what is hidden from you will be disclosed to you. For there is nothing hidden that will not be revealed. [And there is nothing buried that will not be raised.]"

6 His disciples asked him and said to him, "Do you want us to fast? How should we pray? Should we give to charity? What diet should we observe?" Jesus said, "Don't lie, and don't do what you hate, because all things are disclosed before heaven. After all, there is nothing hidden that will not be revealed, and there is nothing covered up that will remain undisclosed."

7 Jesus said, "Lucky is the lion that the human will eat, so that the lion becomes human. And foul is the human that the lion will eat, and the lion still will become human."

8 And he said, the person is like a wise fisherman who cast his net into the sea and drew it up from the sea full of little fish. Among them the wise fisherman discovered a fine large fish. He threw all the little fish back into the sea, and easily chose the large fish. Anyone here with two good ears had better listen!

9 Jesus said, look, the sower went out, took a handful (of seeds), and scattered (them). Some fell on the road, and the birds came and gathered them. Others fell on rock, and they didn't take root in the soil and didn't produce heads of grain. Others fell on thorns, and they choked the seeds and worms ate them. And others fell on good soil, and it produced a good crop: it yielded sixty per measure and one hundred twenty per measure.

10 Jesus said, "I have cast fire upon the world, and look, I'm guarding it until it blazes."

11 Jesus said, "This heaven will pass away, and the one above it will pass away. The dead are not alive, and the living will not die. During the days when you ate what is dead, you made it come alive. When you are in the light, what will you do? On the day when you were one, you became two. But when you become two, what will you do?"

12 The disciples said to Jesus, "We know that you are going to leave us. Who will be our leader?"
Jesus said to them, "No matter where you are you are to go to James the Just, for whose sake heaven and earth came into being."

13 Jesus said to his disciples, "Compare me to something and tell me what I am like." Simon Peter said to him, "You are like a just messenger." Matthew said to him, "You are like a wise philosopher." Thomas said to him, "Teacher, my mouth is utterly unable to say what you are like." Jesus said, "I am not your teacher. Because you have drunk, you have become intoxicated from the bubbling spring that I have tended." And he took him, and withdrew, and spoke three sayings to him. When Thomas came back to his friends they asked him, "What did Jesus say to you?" Thomas said to them, "If I tell you one of the sayings he spoke to me, you will pick up rocks and stone me, and fire will come from the rocks and devour you."

14 Jesus said to them, "If you fast, you will bring sin upon yourselves, and if you pray, you will be condemned, and if you give to charity, you will harm your spirits. When you go into any region and walk about in the countryside, when people take you in, eat what they serve you and heal the sick among them. After all, what goes into your mouth will not defile you; rather, it's what comes out of your mouth that will defile you."

15 Jesus said, "When you see one who was not born of woman, fall on your faces and worship. That one is your Father."

16 Jesus said, "Perhaps people think that I have come to cast peace upon the world. They do not know that I have come to cast conflicts upon the earth: fire, sword, and war. For there will be five in a house: there'll be three against two and two against three, father against son and son against father, and they will stand alone.

17 Jesus said, "I will give you what no eye has seen, what no ear has heard, what no hand has touched, what has not arisen in the human heart."

18 The disciples said to Jesus, "Tell us, how will our end come?"
Jesus said, "Have you found the beginning, then, that you are looking for the end? You see, the end will be where the beginning is. Congratulations to the one who stands at the beginning: that one will know the end and will not taste death."

19 Jesus said, "Congratulations to the one who came into being before coming into being. If you become my disciples and pay attention to my sayings, these stones will serve you. For there are five trees in Paradise for you; they do not change, summer or winter, and their leaves do not fall. Whoever knows them will not taste death."

20 The disciples said to Jesus, "Tell us what Heaven's kingdom is like." He said to them, it's like a mustard seed, the smallest of all seeds, but when it falls on prepared soil, it produces a large plant and becomes a shelter for birds of the sky.

21 Mary said to Jesus, "What are your disciples like?" He said, they are like little children living in a field that is not theirs. when the owners of the field come, they will say, "Give us back our field." They take off their clothes in front of them in order to give it back to them, and they return their field to them. For this reason I say, if the owners of a house know that a thief is coming, they will be on

guard before the thief arrives and will not let the thief break into their house (their domain) and steal their possessions. As for you, then, be on guard against the world. Prepare yourselves with great strength, so the robbers can't find a way to get to you, for the trouble you expect will come. Let there be among you a person who understands. When the crop ripened, he came quickly carrying a sickle and harvested it. Anyone here with two good ears had better listen!

22 Jesus saw some babies nursing. He said to his disciples, "These nursing babies are like those who enter the kingdom." They said to him, "Then shall we enter the kingdom as babies?"
Jesus said to them, "When you make the two into one, and when you make the inner like the outer and the outer like the inner, and the upper like the lower, and when you make male and female into a single one, so that the male will not be male nor the female be female, when you make eyes in place of an eye, a hand in place of a hand, a foot in place of a foot, an image in place of an image, then you will enter [the kingdom]."

23 Jesus said, "I shall choose you, one from a thousand and two from ten thousand, and they will stand as a single one."

24 His disciples said, "Show us the place where you are, for we must seek it." He said to them, "Anyone here with two ears had better listen! There is light within a person of light, and it shines on the whole world. If it does not shine, it is dark."

25 Jesus said, "Love your friends like your own soul, protect them like the pupil of your eye."

26 Jesus said, "You see the sliver in your friend's eye, but you don't see the timber in your own eye. When you take the timber out of your own eye, then you will see well enough to remove the sliver from your friend's eye."

27 "If you do not fast from the world, you will not find the kingdom. If you do not observe the sabbath as a sabbath you will not see the Father."

28 Jesus said, "I took my stand in the midst of the world, and in flesh I appeared to them. I found them all drunk, and I did not find any of them thirsty. My soul ached for the children of humanity, because they are blind in their hearts and do not see, for they came into the world empty, and they also seek to depart from the world empty. But meanwhile they are drunk. When they shake off their wine, then they will change their ways."

29 Jesus said, "If the flesh came into being because of spirit, that is a marvel, but if spirit came into being because of the body, that is a marvel of marvels. Yet I marvel at how this great wealth has come to dwell in this poverty."

30 Jesus said, "Where there are three deities, they are divine. Where there are two or one, I am with that one."

31 Jesus said, "No prophet is welcome on his home turf; doctors don't cure those who know them."

32 Jesus said, "A city built on a high hill and fortified cannot fall, nor can it be hidden."

33 Jesus said, "What you will hear in your ear, in the other ear proclaim from your rooftops. After all, no one lights a lamp and puts it under a basket, nor does one put it in a hidden place. Rather, one puts it on a lamp stand so that all who come and go will see its light."

34 Jesus said, "If a blind person leads a bind person, both of them will fall into a hole."

35 Jesus said, "One can't enter a strong person's house and take it by force without tying his hands. Then one can loot his house."

36 Jesus said, "Do not fret, from morning to evening and from evening to morning, [about your food—what you're going to eat, or about your clothing—] what you are going to wear. [You're much better than the lilies, which neither card nor spin. As for you, when you have no garment, what will you put on? Who might add to your stature? That very one will give you your garment.]"

37 His disciples said, "When will you appear to us, and when will we see you?" Jesus said, "When you strip without being ashamed, and you take your clothes and put them under your feet like little children and trample then, then [you] will see the son of the living one and you will not be afraid."

38 Jesus said, "Often you have desired to hear these sayings that I am speaking to you, and you have no one else from whom to hear them. There will be days when you will seek me and you will not find me."

39 Jesus said, "The Pharisees and the scholars have taken the keys of knowledge and have hidden them. They have not entered nor have they allowed those who want to enter to do so.
As for you, be as sly as snakes and as simple as doves."

40 Jesus said, "A grapevine has been planted apart from the Father. Since it is not strong, it will be pulled up by its root and will perish."

41 Jesus said, "Whoever has something in hand will be given more, and whoever has nothing will be deprived of even the little they have."

42 Jesus said, "Be passersby."

43 His disciples said to him, "Who are you to say these things to us?" "You don't understand who I am from what I say to you. Rather, you have become like the Giddiness, for they love the tree but hate its fruit, or they love the fruit but hate the tree."

44 Jesus said, "Whoever blasphemes against the Father will be forgiven, and whoever blasphemes against the son will be forgiven, but whoever blasphemes against the holy spirit will not be forgiven, either on earth or in heaven."

45 Jesus said, "Grapes are not harvested from thorn trees, nor are figs gathered from thistles, for they yield no fruit. Good persons produce good from what they've stored up; bad persons produce evil from the wickedness they've stored up in their hearts, and say evil things. For from the overflow of the heart they produce evil."

46 Jesus said, "From Adam to John the Baptist, among those born of women, no one is so much greater than John the Baptist that his eyes should not be averted. But I have said that whoever among you becomes a child will recognize the kingdom and will become greater than John."

47 Jesus said, "A person cannot mount two horses or bend two bows. And a slave cannot serve two masters, otherwise that slave will honor the one and offend the other. "Nobody drinks aged wine and immediately wants to drink young wine. Young wine is not poured into old wineskins, or they might break, and aged wine is not poured into a new wineskin, or it might spoil. An old patch is not sewn onto a new garment, since it would create a tear."

48 Jesus said, "If two make peace with each other in a single house, they will say to the mountain, 'Move from here!' and it will move."

49 Jesus said, "Congratulations to those who are alone and chosen, for you will find the kingdom. For you have come from it, and you will return there again."

50 Jesus said, "If they say to you, 'Where have you come from?' say to them, 'We have come from the light, from the place where the light came into being by itself, established [itself], and appeared in their image.' If they say to you, 'Is it you?' say, 'We are its children, and we are the chosen of the living Father.' If they ask you, 'What is the evidence of your Father in you?' say to them, 'It is motion and rest.'"

51 His disciples said to him, "When will the rest for the dead take place, and when will the new world come?" He said to them, "What you are looking forward to has come, but you don't know it."

52 His disciples said to him, "Twenty-four prophets have spoken in Israel, and they all spoke of you." He said to them, "You have disregarded the living one who is in your presence, and have spoken of the dead."

53 His disciples said to him, "is circumcision useful or not?" He said to them, "If it were useful, their father would produce children already circumcised from their mother. Rather, the true circumcision in spirit has become profitable in every respect."

54 Jesus said, "Congratulations to the poor, for to you belongs Heaven's kingdom."

55 Jesus said, "Whoever does not hate father and mother cannot be my disciple, and whoever does not hate brothers and sisters, and carry the cross as I do, will not be worthy of me."

56 Jesus said, "Whoever has come to know the world has discovered a carcass, and whoever has discovered a carcass, of that person the world is not worthy."

57 Jesus said, The Father's kingdom is like a person who has [good] seed. His enemy came during the night and sowed weeds among the good seed. The person did not let the workers pull up the weeds, but said to them, "No, otherwise you might go to pull up the weeds and pull up the wheat along with them." For on

the day of the harvest the weeds will be conspicuous, and will be pulled up and burned.

58 Jesus said, "Congratulations to the person who has toiled and has found life."

59 Jesus said, "Look to the living one as long as you live, otherwise you might die and then try to see the living one, and you will be unable to see."

60 He saw a Samaritan carrying a lamb and going to Judea. He said to his disciples, "that person…around the lamb." They said to him, "So that he may kill it and eat it." He said to them, "He will not eat it while it is alive, but only after he has killed it and it has become a carcass." They said, "Otherwise he can't do it." He said to them, "So also with you, seek for yourselves a place for rest, or you might become a carcass and be eaten."

61 Jesus said, "Two will recline on a couch; one will die, one will live." Salome said, "Who are you mister? You have climbed onto my couch and eaten from my table as if you are from someone." Jesus said to her, "I am the one who comes from what is whole. I was granted from the things of my Father." "I am your disciple."
"For this reason I say, if one is whole, one will be filled with light, but if one is divided, one will be filled with darkness."

62 Jesus said, "I disclose my mysteries to those [who are worthy] of [my] mysteries. Do not let your left hand know what your right hand is doing."

63 Jesus said, There was a rich person who had a great deal of money. He said, "I shall invest my money so that I may sow, reap, plant, and fill my storehouses with produce, that I may lack nothing." These were the things he was thinking in his heart, but that very night he died. Anyone here with two ears had better listen!

64 Jesus said, A person was receiving guests. When he had prepared the dinner, he sent his slave to invite the guests. The slave went to the first and said to that one, "My master invites you." That one said, "Some merchants owe me money; they are coming to me tonight. I have to go and give them instructions. Please excuse me from dinner." The slave went to another and said to that one, "My master has invited you." That one said to the slave, "I have bought a house, and I have been called away for a day. I shall have no time." The slave went to another and said to that one, "My master invites you." That one said to the slave, "My friend is to be married, and I am to arrange the banquet. I shall not be able to

come. Please excuse me from dinner." The slave went to another and said to that one, "My master invites you." That one said to the slave, "I have bought an estate, and I am going to collect the rent. I shall not be able to come. Please excuse me." The slave returned and said to his master, "Those whom you invited to dinner have asked to be excused." The master said to his slave, "Go out on the streets and bring back whomever you find to have dinner." Buyers and merchants [will] not enter the places of my Father.

65 He said, A [...] person owned a vineyard and rented it to some farmers, so they could work it and he could collect its crop from them. He sent his slave so the farmers would give him the vineyard's crop. They grabbed him, beat him, and almost killed him, and the slave returned and told his master. His master said, "Perhaps he didn't know them." He sent another slave, and the farmers beat that one as well. Then the master sent his son and said, "Perhaps they'll show my son some respect." Because the farmers knew that he was the heir to the vineyard, they grabbed him and killed him. Anyone here with two ears had better listen!

66 Jesus said, "Show me the stone that the builders rejected: that is the keystone."

67 Jesus said, "Those who know all, but are lacking in themselves, are utterly lacking."

68 Jesus said, "Congratulations to you when you are hated and persecuted; and no place will be found, wherever you have been persecuted."

69 Jesus said, "Congratulations to those who have been persecuted in their hearts: they are the ones who have truly come to know the Father. Congratulations to those who go hungry, so the stomach of the one in want may be filled."

70 Jesus said, "If you bring forth what is within you, what you have will save you. If you do not have that within you, what you do not have within you [will] kill you."

71 Jesus said, "I will destroy [this] house, and no one will be able to build it [...]."

72 A [person said] to him, "Tell my brothers to divide my father's possessions with me." He said to the person, "Mister, who made me a divider?" He turned to his disciples and said to them, "I'm not a divider, am I?"

73 Jesus said, "The crop is huge but the workers are few, so beg the harvest boss to dispatch workers to the fields."

74 He said, "Lord, there are many around the drinking trough, but there is nothing in the well."

75 Jesus said, "There are many standing at the door, but those who are alone will enter the bridal suite."

76 Jesus said, The Father's kingdom is like a merchant who had a supply of merchandise and found a peal. That merchant was prudent; he sold the merchandise and bought the single pearl for himself. So also with you, seek his treasure that is unfailing, that is enduring, where no moth comes to eat and no worm destroys."

77 Jesus said, "I am the light that is over all things. I am all: from me all came forth, and to me all attained. Split a piece of wood; I am there. Lift up the stone, and you will find me there."

78 Jesus said, "Why have you come out to the countryside? To see a reed shaken by the wind? And to see a person dressed in soft clothes, [like your] rulers and your powerful ones? They are dressed in soft clothes, and they cannot understand truth."

79 A woman in the crowd said to him, "Lucky are the womb that bore you and the breasts that fed you." He said to [her], "Lucky are those who have heard the word of the Father and have truly kept it. For there will be days when you will say, 'Lucky are the womb that has not conceived and the breasts that have not given milk.'"

80 Jesus said, "Whoever has come to know the world has discovered the body, and whoever has discovered the body, of that one the world is not worthy."

81 Jesus said, "Let one who has become wealthy reign, and let one who has power renounce ."

82 Jesus said, "Whoever is near me is near the fire, and whoever is far from me is far from the kingdom."

83 Jesus said, "Images are visible to people, but the light within them is hidden in the image of the Father's light. He will be disclosed, but his image is hidden by his light."

84 Jesus said, "When you see your likeness, you are happy. But when you see your images that came into being before you and that neither die nor become visible, how much you will have to bear!"

85 Jesus said, "Adam came from great power and great wealth, but he was not worthy of you. For had he been worthy, [he would] not [have tasted] death."

86 Jesus said, "[Foxes have] their dens and birds have their nests, but human beings have no place to lay down and rest."

87 Jesus said, "How miserable is the body that depends on a body, and how miserable is the soul that depends on these two."

88 Jesus said, "The messengers and the prophets will come to you and give you what belongs to you. You, in turn, give them what you have, and say to yourselves, 'When will they come and take what belongs to them?'"

89 Jesus said, "Why do you wash the outside of the cup? Don't you understand that the one who made the inside is also the one who made the outside?"

90 Jesus said, "Come to me, for my yoke is comfortable and my lordship is gentle, and you will find rest for yourselves."

91 They said to him, "Tell us who you are so that we may believe in you." He said to them, "You examine the face of heaven and earth, but you have not come to know the one who is in your presence, and you do not know how to examine the present moment.

92 Jesus said, "Seek and you will find.
In the past, however, I did not tell you the things about which you asked me then. Now I am willing to tell them, but you are not seeking them."

93 "Don't give what is holy to dogs, for they might throw them upon the manure pile. Don't throw pearls [to] pigs, or they might...it [...]."

94 Jesus [said], "One who seeks will find, and for [one who knocks] it will be opened."

95 [Jesus said], "If you have money, don't lend it at interest. Rather, give [it] to someone from whom you won't get it back."

96 Jesus [said], The Father's kingdom is like [a] woman. She took a little leaven, [hid] it in dough, and made it into large loaves of bread. Anyone here with two ears had better listen!

97 Jesus said, The [Father's] kingdom is like a woman who was carrying a [jar] full of meal. While she was walking along [a] distant road, the handle of the jar broke and the meal spilled behind her [along] the road. She didn't know it; she hadn't noticed a problem. When she reached her house, she put the jar down and discovered that it was empty.

98 Jesus said, The Father's kingdom is like a person who wanted to kill someone powerful. While still at home he drew his sword and thrust it into the wall to find out whether his hand would go in. Then he killed the powerful one.

99 The disciples said to him, "Your brothers and your mother are standing outside." He said to them, "Those here who do what my Father wants are my brothers and my mother. They are the ones who will enter my Father's kingdom."

100 They showed Jesus a gold coin and said to him, "The Roman emperor's people demand taxes from us." He said to them, "Give the emperor what belongs to the emperor, give God what belongs to God, and give me what is mine."

101 "Whoever does not hate [father] and mother as I do cannot be my [disciple], and whoever does [not] love [father and] mother as I do cannot be my [disciple]. For my mother [...], but my true [mother] gave me life."

102 Jesus said, "Damn the Pharisees! They are like a dog sleeping in the cattle manger: the dog neither eats nor [lets] the cattle eat."

103 Jesus said, "Congratulations to those who know where the rebels are going to attack. [They] can get going, collect their imperial resources, and be prepared before the rebels arrive."

104 They said to Jesus, "Come, let us pray today, and let us fast." Jesus said, "What sin have I committed, or how have I been undone? Rather, when the groom leaves the bridal suite, then let people fast and pray."

105 Jesus said, "Whoever knows the father and the mother will be called the child of a whore."

106 Jesus said, "When you make the two into one, you will become children of Adam, and when you say, 'Mountain, move from here!' it will move."

107 Jesus said, The kingdom is like a shepherd who had a hundred sheep. One of them, the largest, went astray. He left the ninety-nine and looked for the one until he found it. After he had toiled, he said to the sheep, 'I love you more than the ninety-nine.'

108 Jesus said, "Whoever drinks from my mouth will become like me; I myself shall become that person, and the hidden things will be revealed to him."

109 Jesus said, The (Father's) kingdom is like a person who had a treasure hidden in his field but did not know it. And [when] he died he left it to his [son]. The son [did] not know about it either. He took over the field and sold it. The buyer went plowing, [discovered] the treasure, and began to lend money at interest to whomever he wished.

110 Jesus said, "Let one who has found the world, and has become wealthy, renounce the world."

111 Jesus said, "The heavens and the earth will roll up in your presence, and whoever is living from the living one will not see death." Does not Jesus say, "Those who have found themselves, of them the world is not worthy"?

112 Jesus said, "Damn the flesh that depends on the soul. Damn the soul that depends on the flesh."

113 His disciples said to him, "When will the kingdom come?" "It will not come by watching for it. It will not be said, 'Look, here!' or 'Look, there!' Rather, the Father's kingdom is spread out upon the earth, and people don't see it."

APPENDIX C

Reflections on the Gospel of Thomas

As the text for these reflections, I would like to offer a sermon that I preached on May 25, 1997 to the congregation of Summit Unitarian Universalist Fellowship in La Mesa, California. It was a painful time for me, as my bishop, Marcia Herndon, had died a few days before, and I had just been told that she wished me to be her successor as leader of The Thomas Christians. With sadness, love and respect, I began the sermon by dedicating it to her.

My bishop, Marcia Herndon, died this past Monday of liver cancer. I will miss her and my religious community will miss her. She was our Presiding Bishop, and that puts us in no small amount of uncertainty, but I know that she is with us and among us and I take a lot of strength from that. I would like to dedicate my sermon this morning to her memory.

My title this morning is "The Gospel of Thomas and Jesus", and what I hope to do is share the story of this fascinating gospel called The Gospel of Thomas and use it to illustrate the history of my own religious community, known today as The Thomas Christians. I also want to talk about why the discovery of this gospel is so important to contemporary Jesus scholars, and use it to weave out a call to ministry for all religious liberals.

Let us begin by imagining that it's the year 367 A.D. or C.E.—however you like to abbreviate that. Archbishop Athanasius of Alexandria sends out an edict to establish the canonical books of the New Testament. I'm sure that most of you probably know that the New Testament isn't one book that somebody sat down and wrote straight through. It's a collection of a number of books and letters, and it was in 367 that the edict was sent out to bring this collection together and establish a canon.

Now that edict came after a period of a lot of bloody persecution, and the good archbishop would like to avoid more. In his decree he includes a call to condemn all heretical teachings and apocryphal books. Meanwhile, a ways down the Nile, the monks at the Monastery of Saint Paladin get wind of this, and they gather up some documents that are particularly important to them. They stuff them inside an earthenware jar, they seal up the jar, and they bury it in the hills somewhere around their monastery.

Somehow those document survived there. They survived centuries of church councils that subsequently confirmed the canonical New Testament books. Even in those councils the Gospel of Thomas is specifically named as a document to be banned and destroyed. The language they use is pretty strong: "to be damned in the inextricable shackles of anathema forever."

Luckily, our Gospel of Thomas is sealed inside a jar. As far as we know, all the other copies are destroyed. Laying buried as it did, it also escaped redaction as new editions of the canonical texts are copied and recopied over time. It was not at all unheard of for those editors, also called "redactors" to change the text a bit to fit new understandings and even new doctrines.

So, now move forward in time to December 1945. Two brothers are digging in the fields near Nag Hammadi in Egypt. They were looking for a certain kind of soil that was used in the fields as fertilizer. All of a sudden they came across an earthenware jar. They spend a little while arguing about whether or not there's some kind of a whammy attached to it, and then they just can't help themselves, and they break it open. Legend says that when they broke it open, a glistening cloud of golden dust shot up in the air. Well, this glistening cloud of golden dust was probably really, really old papyrus in little tiny pieces that was expelled by the bottle's pressure. After about another fourteen years or so of adventures worthy of a Harrison Ford movie (if you ever read anything about the history of The Gospel of Thomas, it went through this period between 1945 and 1959 of being sold and murdered for and smuggled and hidden from government officials and all split up into different pieces, but after a while it's finally compiled and photographed). Finally, the Gospel of Thomas is seen for the first time and interpreted by scholars.

The version of The Gospel of Thomas that we have today was most likely written in about the year 350, although we have older Greek fragments found that have been dated about 200. Scholars believe the original was written, possibly by a contemporary of Thomas, around 50 or 60; and that, of course, would put the writing of it within one generation of Jesus' life and death, making them the oldest gospels extant. That's really important when we consider the content and the length. The length of The Gospel of Thomas could probably fit on two double-side pieces of paper. It's very short, and it's a gospel of short sayings, all of them beginning, usually, with "Jesus said." That is significant, because that's almost exactly what the "Q" document looks like, and let me briefly tell you about Q.

The "Q" document is a historical document that's been hypothesized by modern Bible scholars. They believe it was the document that was used to write what we now know as the Synoptic Gospels—Matthew, Mark, and Luke. It too is a short document, can fit on two sides of two pieces of paper, and is a document of sayings. What is really interesting about all this, of course, is what's not in either of these documents: what's not in the "Q" document and what's not in The Gospel of Thomas. There is no virgin birth, there is no resurrection, and there are no miracles. There is hardly a breath about sin and suffering. Jesus never claims to be the Son of God. He heals, he visits, he feeds, and he frees. And he is unconditionally inclusive.

In his book, "The Essential Jesus", Bible scholar and theologian Dominic Crossan describes Jesus' mission, based on these texts, as, and I quote, "A program of empowerment for a peasantry becoming steadily more hard-pressed through incessant taxation, attendant indebtedness, and eventual land expropriation.

Against this systemic injustice and structural evil, Jesus lived an alternative open to all who would accept it—a life of open healing and shared eating, of radical itinerancy, of programmatic homelessness and fundamental egalitarianism, of human contact without discrimination, and of divine contact without hierarchy. He also died for that alternative. That is my understanding of what Jesus' words and deeds were all about." That is a radically different understanding of Jesus than the one that we have been spoon-fed for two thousand years, and we can see why some church fathers might want these documents burned.

These people who used the Gospel of Thomas, who read it, who used it in their worship, who were they? The indigenous Christians of India, that is to say not Roman Catholics brought to India by Jesuits in the sixteenth century or Protestants brought there by the British include several flavors of what was called the ancient Syrian church, and was thought to have been started by the Apostle Thomas himself. Even today this tradition survives in the Orthodox Church of Thomas along the Malabar Coast. These Christians assert that Thomas came there, again, between 50 and 60, and established a church; and The Gospel of Thomas has always been a part of their oral tradition, even though they didn't have a written copy until it was found in 1945. Again, I think that lends a fair amount of credibility, since their oral traditions and the actual Gospel of Thomas turn out to be so similar.

A little more relevant to my own religious community is that an English Unitarian named Ulric Vernon Herford went to visit those Christians in India in 1905. He was seeking to start a church in apostolic succession that would be ecumenical and that would set itself up against the structural, institutional churches of his time. (In England, of course, the Roman Catholic Church and the Church of England, the Anglicans.) He considered this early Thomas church to be the true church, and they consecrated him so that he could start a similar church in the West. He continued his ministry in England until he died, mostly a social justice ministry, as that was what he thought the focus of the historical Jesus' message was. He ordained priests and bishops who eventually gave their blessing to a radical bishop named Mikhail Itkin to continue his community in America, and that's how the community that I belong to began.

It survives in England even today as the British Orthodox Church, and here in America as The Thomas Christians. Our small order still defines our ministry using the ancients as our guide, and so the religious community that I belong to tries to live our religious life without any doctrine or dogma or hierarchy. Our ministry is as itinerants instead of building institutions. We're very careful not to limit the definition of family, which Jesus certainly did not do. And, in fact, we are especially valuing of extended family units, that being both biological families and families that gather together for other reasons. We try not to confuse financial gain with ministry, as the entire modern church has managed to do. We ask for what's needed. We try not to make our ritual and worship more important than our ministry. We have minimal organization. And, finally, we are radically inclusive. When The Gospel of Thomas was written, that meant the full inclusion of women. Today it means the full inclusion of anyone who is on the margins.

The discovery of the Gospel of Thomas has some special importance for modern scholarship. I know a lot of you are probably familiar with the Jesus Seminar, a large group of scholars who've come together to try to determine what Jesus actually did say and what Jesus actually did do. Their continuing work points to the idea of Christianity as panentheism, that is a God that is not only transcendent but a God that is within and among.

The author Stephen Mitchell's work points to this in his book "The Gospel According to Jesus". I'm going to read a little bit from that in a second. Again, he redefines this ministry of Jesus from the message we've all heard over the centuries. He peels away all the layers of theology that have weighed down this message, and it's powerful. It is no surprise at all that modern churches have put enormous energy into discrediting the Jesus Seminar, into writing books against the Jesus Seminar, to making sure that Jesus Seminar speakers are not allowed important professorships around the country, making sure Jesus Seminar members are not allowed important pulpits around the country, and making sure that Jesus Seminar scholars are not allowed important speaking engagements around the country.

Let me share a very short paragraph from Mitchell and his conclusion about some of the importance of this early Jesus work: *"The kingdom of God is not something that will happen, because it isn't something that can happen. It can't appear in a world or nation. It is a condition that has no plural but only infinite singulars. Jesus spoke of people entering it, said that children were already inside it, told one particularly ardent scribe that he, the scribe, was not far from it. If only we stop looking forward and backward, he said, we'll be able to devote ourselves to seeking the kingdom of God, which is right beneath our feet, right under our noses, and when we find it food, clothing, and other necessities are given to us as well, as they are to the birds and to the lilies. Where else but the here and now can we find grace bestowing the inexhaustible presence of God? In its light all hopes and fears fritter away like ghosts. It is like a treasure buried in a field. It is like a pearl of great price. It is like coming home. When we find it, we find ourselves: rich beyond all dreams, and we realize that we can afford to lose everything else in the world. Even, if we must, someone we love more dearly than life itself."*

I think the message of The Gospel of Thomas and the new Jesus scholarship that weaves out of it is a fascinating call to ministry for religious liberals. It turns out that the faithful who come together in community like this and who value the social gospel or ministry as service are probably the ones that have it right. Thankfully, I think, many churches do have a respectable record here, and I want to extend a special word to my brother and sister Roman Catholics because they have put a great deal of their financial and human resource energies into social justice ministry, in spite of all the other things that they have done that I might find anathema. Of course, so do most communities of religious liberals and we can be proud of that. As I've said from this pulpit before, our record of service is totally out of proportion to our small numbers. Heal, visit, feed, and free: that has been the message of the social gospel. We should all be proud that we have embraced that message.

I also think this gospel story is important to religious liberals in a few other ways. For one, it gives us a reason to start thinking about taking the Bible back. I don't mean to hammer on it, but the fact is that religious liberals have given up the Bible to the fundamentalists and everybody else who wants to define it in their own very narrow ways when, in fact, this is a document that we should be talking about as exemplifying the mission that we are on; to build interfaith community. We need to take it back. It belongs to us, too.

When I think about genuine liberal religious community, I think immediately of the Gospel of Thomas, because so many liberal principles are affirmed, such as the affirmation of the dignity and worth of every person, Jesus' call for justice and compassion, being a radically inclusive community, being open to growth, and affirming conscience and group process as guiding principles. It also affirms our respect for the interdependent web of all life. Something, it turns out, that Jesus really did know something about. This is the Gospel of Thomas, saying number three: Jesus said, "If your leaders say to you, Look, the Creator's Imperial Rule is in the sky,' then the birds of the sky will precede you. If they say to you, It is in the sea,' then the fish will precede you. Rather, the Creator's Imperial Rule is within you and is outside you. When you know yourselves, then you will be known, and you will understand that you are children of the living God."

My vision of holiness is a world where religious differences are celebrated. Those of us who are Thomasine, small as we are, will continue to build upon our own spirituality and try to bring forward the real message of Jesus. Wouldn't it be ironic, in this puritanical day and age, if it was the historical Jesus who called across the centuries to bring us into new community? Wouldn't it be ironic if it was the historical Jesus who taught us to finally celebrate all of our differences? Wouldn't it be ironic if it was the historical Jesus who helped us all see, of whatever religion, the compassion for others and our planet that is living deep inside all of our hearts?

In the name of the living God: Creator, Liberator, and Great Spirit, Amen.

Appendix D

Herford and Itkin Biographies

Vernon Herford

Ulric Vernon Herford was born on November 16, 1866, the third son of William Henry Herford, a Unitarian minister and educational reformer. Herford studied at Owens College, Manchester, from 1886 to 1889, and later attended Manchester College, Oxford, in preparation for the Unitarian ministry. In 1891, the liturgically inclined seminarian left Manchester College for St. Stephen's House, an Anglican school of theology in Oxford, for a year's study.

Long identified with "orthodox" or Christian Unitarianism, Herford published "The Hymnal" in 1892. It was a collection of over two hundred and fifty hymns, selected by Herford for use by Unitarian as well as Trinitarian Christians. From 1893 to 1896, he ministered to a small Unitarian Chapel in Norfolk, and later was named to pastor a church in Shropshire. He returned to Oxford in 1897 to minister to a small congregation at the College. Herford was quite happy there, as the community was—like him—only nominally Unitarian.

One year later Herford was called to pastor the newly opened Church of the Divine Love, a red brick building in a poor neighborhood over Magdalen Bridge, on Oxford's east side. There, Herford spent his days ministering to the poor and tending a small garden with a group of young men from the congregation.

Herford and the "Brothers," as he half-jokingly called them, modeled themselves after the monastic ideal. The people of Oxford's east side flocked to Herford's church to hear the Unitarian monk preach with apostolic zeal against all manner of personal and social evil.

Over time, Herford developed a rule for his small semi-monastic community, which he dubbed the Order of the Christian Faith (O.C.F.). Beginning in 1900 the Order published several issues of a magazine called "The Christian Churchman." But the O.C.F. never developed into the self-supporting community Herford had envisioned. After only a year, the Order was all but defunct.

But the spirit of the Order lived on. Herford saw the O.C.F. as a genuinely ecumenical brotherhood dedicated to the unity of all Christians—Unitarian and Trinitarian, Catholic and Protestant, East and West. By 1902, the congregants at the Church of the Divine Love had become decidedly high church in their worship, uncharacteristic for a Unitarian congregation, even an avowedly Christian one. Spurred on by this new spirit of liturgical innovation, Herford wrote a series of articles and sermons in which he described his vision of an ecumenical, and genuinely liturgical, Christian church.

On July 6, 1902, Herford preached one of the most important sermons of his life to the Unitarian Sunday School Teachers' Summer School at Oxford. He explained the genesis of the O.C.F. to an assembly of Unitarian teachers and ministers, and told his hearers that the Order had been "an awakening from [a] slothful condition of drift to realize that we were called of God to be the germ of the great all-embracing Church of the future, meeting all the spiritual needs of man, with sacraments of grace for the heart and will, as well as sermons for the intellect." He invited his co-religionists to place themselves "into the stream of a great common faith," and to return to the heart of true Christianity.

Herford had already taken concrete steps in this direction, writing to those whom he regarded as "the purest and most primitive Branch of the Holy Catholic and Apostolic Church"—the East Syrian or Syro-Chaldean Church, which claimed St. Thomas the Apostle as its founder. In his first of many letters to Mar Basilius (Luis Mariano Suares), the Syro-Chaldean Metropolitan (February 27, 1902), he requested information about the church and suggested an alliance, noting the similarities between his own form of Unitarian Christianity and what had traditionally been called Nestorianism, a Christological doctrine of the 5th century which held that "the manhood is the face of the Godhead, and the Godhead is the face of the manhood."

The British had first made contact with the Nestorians during archaeological digs at the sites of several Assyrian monuments in the early part of the nineteenth-century, and English interest was again later sparked by news of terrible massacres of Nestorians by Kurds in 1831, 1843 and 1846. As a direct result of these atrocities, the Archbishop of Canterbury's Mission to the Assyrian Christians was founded. It was officially established, with full church funding and sanction, in 1886. Canterbury opened schools and provided printing presses for liturgical books. A translation project was also begun, and English versions of Nestorian prayers and liturgies were made available to the British reading public. Herford's acquaintance with Nestorian Christianity was contemporary with the work of the Assyrian Mission.

Mar Basilius, the Bishop who would eventually consecrate Herford to the episcopacy, was once Fr. Luis Mariano Soares, formerly "a Roman Catholic cleric of Goa, of Brahmin descent," as he was described by Herford. Later he was ordained a priest by Mar Julius (Alvarez) of the Independent Catholic Church of Ceylon, himself consecrated by the Jacobite Thomas Christians of India. Later, Soares was elected to the episcopacy by a body of Indian Christians in Madura who had risen up against what they saw as inhumane treatment received at the hands of Jesuit missionaries. This small group petitioned Mar Abd-Tshu (Abed-Jesus) to consecrate Soares, which he did on "the twenty-third of Tammuz 1899 of the Christian Era, in the great Chaldean Church of the Cathedral City of Trichur," assisted by Mar Agostinos, Bishop of Trichur. At his consecration Luis Mariano Soares became Mar Basilius. Mar Abd-Tshu (once Thondanatta Antony) had been consecrated in the early 1860s by the Nestorian Patriarch of Babylon (see G. T. MacKenzie, "Christianity in Travancore").

In April of 1902, Herford provided Mar Basilius with a catechism, in English and Latin, which he had prepared for his congregants and for those interested in his liturgical renewal of Unitarian Christianity. Accompanying the catechism was a request: "If you and another bishop with you could come to England, we should be very happy to entertain you if you would consecrate to the episcopal office two of us in order to establish a Church in England in union with the Nestorian Church."

On May 27, 1902, Mar Basilius responded favorably to Herford's request: "Gladly I would give the Episcopal office to both of you, because the Episcopate is not our private Patrimony," he wrote. "As freely as we have received it from the Divine Church, we are bound to distribute freely amongst the needy, commanding only, 'Attendite vobis, et universo gregi in quo vos Spiritus Sanctus posuit Episcopus, regere ecclesiam Dei Quam acquisivit sanguine suo" (Acts XX.28).

On the Feast of St. Andrew, 1902, a solemn ceremony of consecration was conducted at the Church of the Epiphany at Palithamem, India. Mar Basilius had Herford recite the East Syrian creed (which Herford described in a letter to an Anglican newspaper as "the only Ecumenical Creed) and, during a solemn liturgy, named him Mar Jacobus, Bishop of Mercia. Later, Herford wrote an official letter to Mar Shimun (Simon) XIX, Patriarch of Seleucia-Ctesiphon and Katholikos of the East (murdered by the Turks in 1917), informing him of Mar Basilius's actions and pledging the "loyal homage of myself and all the faithful under my jurisdiction in England." He enclosed a copy of the Act of Consecration and the Staticon of Jurisdiction. On December 11, 1903, by Deed Poll, and duly enrolled in the Supreme Court of England, Herford legally assumed the name, "Mar Jacobus, Bishop of Mercia," in addition to his surname.

Herford was already widely known as a reformer, and a fighter on behalf of the rights of the poor. He agitated to extend the Parliamentary vote to women, argued against oppressive rents, and called for investigations of child labor practices in the sweatshops of London. He regarded the Boer War as a scandal at a time when the South African campaign was widely touted by "patriots" as a worthy show of British imperial might.

On January 17, 1907, Herford married Alice Skerritt of Hove, an Anglican with Free Church sympathies. Though she loved Herford dearly, she was suspicious of his interests in Eastern Christianity, and his status as Bishop of Mercia. However, she did share Herford's passion for animal rights, and worked alongside him in the Oxford Anti-Vivesection Society. Together they canvassed on behalf of the cause.

In 1908, Herford met Bishop Arnold Harris Mathew, and the two became fast friends. Herford not only showed great interest in the Old Catholics of Holland, but expressed his (qualified) adhesion to the principles set down in the Declaration of Utrecht. Herford even visited Holland, where he held conversations with several Bishops and clergy.

Herford was also quite sympathetic to the form of French "liberal" Catholicism begun by the Abbe Robert de Lamennais in the nineteenth-century and a supporter of Fr. George Tyrrell, the apostle of Roman Catholic modernism in the English-speaking world. Tyrrell's untimely death in 1909 prevented Herford from implementing his plan for cooperation with Tyrrell and the British supporters of his party. Eventually, the Bishop of Mercia's See came to be known as the Evangelical Catholic Church. He published a revised book of prayers and liturgies, known as the "Euchologion" (later reprinted by Basil Blackwell in 1920).

During World War I, Herford remained a staunch pacifist. He worked with members of the newly formed Fellowship of Reconciliation, the Anti-Conscription Committee in Oxford, and the Society of Friends. Every Wednesday afternoon during the war, Herford held Services of Intercession for the cause of peace. He joined the Fellowship of Reconciliation and remained a member for the rest of his life.

After the war, Herford resumed his theological and pastoral writing, penning a new Confession of Faith for the Evangelical Catholic Church, and numerous essays, among them "Jesus Christ is the Sacrament of God." His ecumenical work continued in force as he made contacts with the Anglican Benedictine Community at Pershore Abbey, Worcestershire, the Society of Jesus (despite their steady persecution of the Syro-Chaldean Church in India), Congregationalists, and clergy and laity from other confessions.

An Evangelical Catholic Mission was established at Burton-on-Trent, Staffordshire, in the 1920s. It was founded by a layman, Ernest Cope, and originally known as St. James Guild, a "house church" in the style of the free and peace churches, dedicated to the work of Christian unity. Eventually, Cope made contact with Bishop Herford, and requested his oversight and guidance. The guild became St. John's Christian Mission at Stapenhill. Herford instructed the members of the Mission in the Liturgy of St. Sarapion, and he later assigned Fr. G.C. Batten to the mission church. Herford performed St. John's first confirmations on Sunday, February 3, 1929.

As the ECC continued to grow, Herford ordained several more men to the priesthood, among them T. E. Pickering, an active labor and unemployment demonstrator often mentioned in the daily press. Herford consecrated one Bishop, W. S. McBean Knight, in 1925 as Bishop of Kent. Later, Bishop McBean Knight consecrated Hedley Coward Bartlett to the episcopacy in 1931, thus providing for the continuity of the ECC lineage in England.

The Bishop's wife, Alice Skerritt Herford, passed away on March 13, 1928, after a long illness. A solemn requiem was celebrated in Oxford and attended by friends and members of Herford's parish. Herford withdrew somewhat, and only for a time, from active parish ministry, editing and writing for his new venture, "The Church and Chapel Parish Magazine," an ecumenical journal for people in the various free church traditions. It was a magazine dedicated to applied Christianity, and widely circulated.

In 1931 Herford published the "Catechism of Evangelical Catholic Doctrine, for Christians who refuse to recognize any real division in the One great Church of Jesus Christ." There were 173 Questions and Answers, dealing with everything from the nature of the Godhead to grace, prayer and charity. Four forms of the Creed were set out, the most ancient being the Apology of Aristides (c. 150 AD). By 1934 Herford was attempting to revive the O.C.F. Rule. To this end, he wrote an essay titled, "The Modern Value of Franciscanism," which was published in the F.o.R. magazine, "Reconciliation" (November, 1934). It read, in part, "As Europe was won to Christianity not by preachers and books so much as by the monastic communities, silently setting the example of profound faith in the objectivity of God, worship, Christian communism and real brotherhood, so might small groups of real Franciscans form religious families of unmarried men…"

In April of 1938, Herford remembered the Fortieth Anniversary of the opening of the Church of the Divine Love. During the summer of that year he was a visible and highly active participant in the F.o.R. Conference at Derbyshire, and traveled from there to Manchester and Scotland. After a brief illness, Herford died sometime during the late night hours of Monday, August 15 or the early morning hours of Tuesday, the 16th. His obituary in the "Oxford Mail" was as gentle and whimsical as the man it described. It closed with the words, "Bishop Herford was well known in Oxford, where he was often seen riding a bicycle and wearing a shoulder cape."

Mikhail Itkin

Michael Lewis Itkin was born on February 7, 1936, in New York City. Both his parents were Jewish, and his father was a Russian immigrant. He was raised in the tumultuous environment of depression and wartime New York, and was enthralled by the variety of political and religious activities available to him. At various times he was involved with such disparate organizations as the Communist Party USA, and the Jehovah's Witnesses, among many others. Such was the nature of his never ending search for new knowledge and experience, likely reflected in the presumption that he had ADHD and bipolar disorder. His parent's experience and influence must have played a part as well.

At the age of sixteen, Michael was ordained a minister for the People's Institute of Applied Religion/The Way, an organization committed to social activism. Two years later, on June 16, 1954, Michael was baptized into The Episcopal Church.

In the early fifties, Michael became aware of his homosexuality, and experienced the bashing and persecution, both individual and institutional, that this brought him. He was torn between his love of the drama of the liturgy, especially the eucharist, and the traditional stand on sexuality taught in the churches he attended. Then he heard of the Eucharistic Catholic Church.

This Independent Catholic body, under the direction of Bishop George Hyde, is claimed by some to have been the first gay-centered religious body in the United States. The church had been founded in 1946 with an inclusive ministry that specifically welcomed gay men and lesbians into membership. Already interested in a liturgically centered spirituality, Michael was enchanted with this catholic church. He joined the church, became active in worship and study, and was ordained a priest by Bishop Hyde on May 6, 1957. It was around this time that Michael began using the Russian version of his name, Mikhail.

Always willing to defy the institutional structure, Father Mikhail felt his superiors were not moving fast enough on social issues. He worked hard at developing a ministry that was both open to gays and lesbians as well as deeply committed to pacifism and social justice. Over time he began to develop a small base community of followers, and which gradually moved away from Bishop Hyde's organization. After meeting another bishop and seeking to move forward with his own community, Mikhail was consecrated a bishop by Carl Jerome Stanley on November 12, 1960. His scattered nature and inability to settle down led him to change his small group's name frequently, which matched the rapid evolution of his theological thought. Mikhail was conditionally consecrated eight more times during his life, in an attempt to build an "ecumenical" episcopate.

Although he had little formal education, Mikhail was a voracious reader, and most of his peers considered him quite brilliant. Most of his peers also considered him somewhat unstable, and because of his manic-depression he collected SSI disability benefits for most of his adult life. Eventually, he founded the Evangelical Catholic Community of the Love of Christ, which in the form of The Thomas Christians continues today. He also authored a pivotal work in gay-centered theology, The Radical Jesus and Gay Liberation", in 1972.

Throughout his adult life, Mikhail had very few steady constants. One was the Community of the Love of Christ. His other great interest was the early 20th century work of Bishop Ulric Vernon Herford. He felt a deep connection to this historical Independent Catholic figure, and believed he was connected to him though the tradition of apostolic succession. While this claim is doubtful, it is certainly true that Herford's successors gave their blessing to Mikhail to continue Herford's work in the United States. For Mikhail, this gave even more meaning to his own inner call to the causes of peace and justice.

Bishop Itkin's many contributions to the cause of inclusion, peace, and justice include authoring the resolution on gay rights adopted by the American Sociological Association, the first such resolution adopted by an American scholarly or professional association. He co-founded the Committee of Concern for Homosexuals that established the first Gay Switchboard in the San Francisco bay area, where he had finally settled in the late seventies. He also celebrated a weekly eucharist at the AIDS Vigil held in San Francisco in the early to mid 1980's.

Bishop Mikhail Itkin died of complications of AIDS on August 1, 1989. His funeral mass was held at St. John's Episcopal Church in San Francisco on August 12, 1989. Participants described it as "all the grandeur of a full pontifical mass, with clouds of incense and heaven-bound hymns and prayers". The homilist was Mikhail's chosen successor as leader of his community, The Most Reverend Marcia Herndon. Bishop Herndon herself succumbed to cancer in 1997, and Donald Bruce Stouder was chosen to succeed her. Among the congregation at Mikhail's funeral were representatives of the city government, San Francisco's gay community, and ministers from several denominations and others who had been touched in some way by the life of Bishop Mikhail Itkin.

As a part of the service, participants were invited to speak about the bishop. A number in succession volunteered that "Mikhail was a pain in the butt". But each quickly added that all his life Mikhail was in the forefront of social concern. His advocacy of the rights of the poor and disenfranchised, of women, of racial and sexual minorities was constant and unwavering. For his efforts he suffered persecution and ridicule.

Most who spoke freely acknowledged Mikhail often did not seem to know where he was going, and stories of sexual indiscretions circulated just below the surface. It seemed that because of this uncertainty or indecision he often ended up in places that he did not want to be. His correspondence and journals are filled with backtracking and "corrections", and explanations of earlier statements of position, frequently accompanied by bitter denunciations of those who still held these now repudiated positions. But it was just as freely acknowledged by his impromptu eulogists that he always tried to go toward the good. All agreed he always tried to serve God and humanity.

Bishop Itkin had suffered the ravages of AIDS for several years, even while watching so many of his friends succumb to the illness. Still, he seemed to know what lay ahead for him, as is illustrated in this 1983 excerpt from his personal journal: "I returned from the annual Memorial Service for Harvey Milk and George Moscone at Grace Cathedral last night to find Edric (his cat) ill, and soon became quite ill myself. Vomiting and diarrhea kept me up much of the night. Through this illness, in which I feel myself ripped apart, there are still occasional moments of incredible light. I know what Goethe desired on his deathbed, calling for light! more light!, but it is not mine yet."

"I have the memory of an earlier vision, and it must suffice for now. The Christ himself, our Lord Jesus, appeared to me, both suffering and glorified, and told me he has saved the whole creation, even me. It is enough. God has blessed me and I should be satisfied."

About the Author

Donald B. Stouder is a certified life coach, experienced spiritual counselor, the CEO of Life Coaching of San Diego, and is the Director of the Center for Spiritual Care at Sharp Grossmont Hospital as well as serving as co-chair of the hospital's Medical Ethics Committee. A former paramedic, Don is a Unitarian Universalist minister, and has been working in the field of professional chaplaincy for over eleven years. Holding a masters degree in religion and having completed a 24 month hospital residency in crisis counseling, Don is certified by the American Association of Pastoral Counselors as a Pastoral Care Specialist, and has completed advanced training in health care ethics at the University of Washington in Seattle and Emory University in Atlanta. He is the author or co-author of 5 books, and is a frequent speaker and educator on subjects related to spiritual care, cultural awareness, religion and healing, and bioethics throughout the San Diego community.

Don's academic interests span the realm of religion and psychology, from the convergence of east/west spiritual philosophies in psychology and health to the use of holistic and alternative modalities with patients and families. Since joining the faculty of San Diego University for Integrative Studies in the spring of 2003, he has taught courses in East/West Psychology, Theories of Consciousness, Counseling Issues with HIV Positive Clients, and Buddhist Bioethics. Don will participate in the Summer 2004 Transpersonal Psychology Intensive with an offering titled "Therapeutic Uses of the Labyrinth". Don has been a member of numerous community organizations and boards, and was nominated for the Sharp HealthCare Spirit of Caring Award in 2001. He is currently at work on a Ph.D. in transpersonal psychology.

To Contact The Author

don@lifecoachsandiego.com
www.lifecoachsandiego.com

0-595-31862-2